"A fresh heartfelt book. *Wonderland* is down t[...] [...]d unique. Silberberg explores what contemporar[...] [...]e to the fundamentals and essence of the teach[...]
>   —Genpo Merzel Roshi, founder and teacher of Kanzeon International and author of *Big Mind—Big Heart: Finding Your Way*

"Doen Silberberg collaborates with Lewis Carroll, producing a very readable and personal account of the spiritual journey. *Wonderland* is a valuable place to enter the Buddhist teachings."
>   —John Daido Loori Roshi, author of *Heart of Being*, abbot of Zen Mountain Monastery and founder of the Mountains and Rivers Order

"A wise and rich vision of the dharma, unusual, psychologically astute, a must-read."
>   —Joan Halifax, head teacher, Upaya Zen Center

"Daniel Silberberg shows us that our life at this moment—whether ordered and familiar as Alice's was or confused and unsettling as it came to be—is just exactly perfect. It is itself Wonderland."
>   —Matthew Bortolin, author of *The Dharma of Star Wars*

"Like Baba Ram Dass and the late Carlos Castaneda, Daniel Doen Silberberg Sensei has the ability to present the eternal journey of self-discovery in a way that's entertaining, personal, and deeply insightful."
>   —Jeremy Silman, international chess master and author of 38 books including *How to Reassess Your Chess* and *Zen and the Art of Casino Gaming*

"Words are a music, more often than not formed to avoid 'the dance.' Read these words, if you will, and you might hear a deeper music and find yourself dancing. Doen's work is a wonderfully cogent, gentle, and incisive journey 'down the hole.'"
>   —Robert Berky, award-winning theatrical clown, actor, director, and playwright

"Daniel Doen Silberberg has one of the clearest, most compelling voices in Zen. He demystifies esoteric teachings in an authentic, fresh way for real people who live real lives. It is impossible to read his work and not feel that something inside you has profoundly changed."
>   —Julie Reiser, Johns Hopkins University

Parallax Press is committed to preserving ancient forests and natural resources. This book is printed on Rolland Enviro 100 Book recycled paper (100 percent post-consumer recycled paper, processed chlorine free). Using 2,242 pounds of this paper instead of virgin fibers paper saved:

19 trees, 1,211 lbs of solid waste
(equivalent of 0.4 American football fields)

11,430 gallons of water
(equivalent of a shower of 2.4 days)

7.7 lbs of suspended particles in water

2,659 lbs of air emissions
(equivalent of emissions of 0.2 cars per year)

2,771 ft³ of natural gas

Wonderland

THE ZEN OF ALICE

Wonderland

THE ZEN OF ALICE

DANIEL

DOEN

SILBERBERG

PARALLAX PRESS
BERKELEY, CA

Parallax Press
P.O. Box 7355
Berkeley, California 94707

Parallax Press is the publishing division of
Unified Buddhist Church, Inc.

Cover design by Robin Terra.
Text design by Paami Disston.

The Heart Sutra excerpts in the Introduction and Chapters 3, 7, and 8 are
from a translation handed down through the lineage that eventually became the
Mountains and Rivers Order of Zen Buddhism (www.mro.org). The Diamond
Sutra in the Introduction and Chapter 3 is excerpted from *The Clear Light
Series*, translated by A. F. Price and Wong Mou-Lam (Boulder, CO: Shambhala
Publications, Inc., 1969). The quotes in Chapter 6 are taken from *The Buddha
Speaks*, Anne Bancroft, ed. (Boston, MA: Shambhala Publications, Inc., 2000).
The quotes in Chapter 7 are taken from *The Blue Cliff Record*, translated by
Thomas Cleary (Boston, MA: Shambhala Publications, Inc., 2005). Quotes from
the Shobogenzo are from "Moon in a Dewdrop," edited by Kazuaki Tanahashi
(San Francisco Zen Center, 1985). All quotations from *Alice's Adventures in
Wonderland* by Lewis Carroll are from The Millennium Fulcrum Edition 2.7
of the Project Gutenberg electronic text.

Library of Congress Cataloging-in-Publication Data

Silberberg, Daniel Doen, 1947-
Wonderland : the Zen of Alice / Daniel Doen Silberberg.

    p. cm.

Includes bibliographical references.
ISBN 978-1-888375-95-4

1. Zen Buddhism. 2. Alice (Fictitious character : Carroll) I. Carroll, Lewis,
1832-1898. Alice's Adventures in Wonderland. II. Title.

    BQ9266.S54 2009
    294.3'927—dc22   2009013972

1 2 3 4 5 / 13 12 11 10 09

TABLE OF CONTENTS

Zen takes us beyond concepts, words, and ideas, allowing us to see deeply into the nature of reality and who we truly are. The history of Zen is full of skillful means to aid this process, including the use of words to transcend words. Poems, stories, koans, dialogues between teachers and students, and talks by living masters are all examples of Zen's tradition of using words to transcend words.

One notable example of the literary culture of Zen is the "Zenrin Kushu"—Phrases from a Zen Forest. Most of these phrases are derived from Chinese poetry. These poems, sayings, and stories represent the cultural understanding of another time and place. They rely on the readers' shared culture and shared body of knowledge. As Zen lands on Western shores and begins to permeate our culture, we can benefit from stories, songs, and poems we in the West share in order to communicate its teachings. We have to look to our own culture, to the richness of our own associations; otherwise we wind up studying something exotic, of another place and time, something not ours.

Now is the right time to make Zen ours, to make it strong and true. Lewis Carroll's *Alice's Adventures in Wonderland* is the story Doen Sensei uses as his aid in this book. We share his and Alice's experiences of falling into a magic hole and finding "Wonderland," a place that is unknowable, where our everyday conditioning no longer applies. It is an adventure in reality, as this book itself is part of the adventure of establishing the foundation for a truly Western Zen, yet still true to its Eastern origins and wisdom. It is my hope that after some time passes, Zen will be so deeply rooted in Western culture that it will not be unusual to associate the things we hold in common, our stories, with the practice of Zen. This book is a great step in that direction. I hope your adventures with Doen Sensei's creative teachings help you appreciate this world, this Wonderland. I am very pleased and honored to participate in offering his teachings to the world.

Genpo Merzel Roshi
Salt Lake City, Utah
April 2009

Ejo studied with Zen Master Dogen. One day in the course of inquiries he heard the saying, "One hair goes through the myriad holes" and all of a sudden realized enlightenment.

That evening he went to Dogen and said, "I do not ask about the one hair, what about the myriad holes?" Dogen smiled and said, "Gone through." Ejo bowed.

—The Denkoroku

"What matters it how far we go?" his scaly friend replied.

"There is another shore, you know, upon the other side.

The further off from England the nearer is to France—

Then turn not pale, beloved snail, but come and join the dance.

Will you, won't you, will you, won't you, will you join the dance?

Will you, won't you, will you, won't you, won't you join the dance?"

—*Alice's Adventures in Wonderland* by Lewis Carroll

Alice fell down a hole. Like many people she was quite sure she was on solid ground; that is, until she wasn't. She didn't fall down an ordinary hole, but a door into another world. As we follow Alice's adventures on the other side of the door, we get the feeling that her previous life was a bit mannered, prescribed, and, well, boring. After she falls down the rabbit hole, everything changes. The rules take a sharp turn, invert, and fade like a Cheshire cat's smile. Nothing is ever the same again for Alice or for the reader.

The way of Zen can also take us for a spin, creating a special kind of internal dissonance where the familiar harmonies and music don't come as expected. It's not that dissonance isn't harmony; it's just a different kind of harmony. To experience the truth and beauty of dissonant music, Alice has to give up her expectations and accept what is. If, like Alice, we give up our expectations, we may find that we can hear and see an alternative truth as well. We may even see ourselves clearly for the first time.

In her journey, Alice experiences all sorts of wondrous things and has conversations with extraordinary characters. She meets talking cards, flamingos that are mallets, a bloodthirsty queen, and a disappearing cat. This world—which Alice finds so unfamiliar, unpredictable, and outrageous—is Wonderland.

In our own lives, wonder is easily misplaced or lost. We forget that this vast unknowable world and our own lives can never be reduced to polite logic. In the Diamond Sutra, the Buddha says, "This world is not a world; and so is provisionally called a world." Our conclusions and concepts cover the truth of our world. Peeling the crust off our old concept of the world is a journey, a joy, and a practice. Like Alice, we can all find a way that is wondrously lost, that has heart, and that rings true.

The Buddha spoke a lot about "the other shore," a place where illusions fall away and we can see the world clearly. In Zen practice, at the end of the Heart Sutra we chant: "Gone to the other shore: gone, gone to the other shore." The other shore is the realm where body and mind fall away and we see that we're one with everything. It's often been thought of as elsewhere, in the future, both historically and in our lives. Many of us want to get there and concoct schemes and plans for reaching it. But it is nothing other than this moment, this life, this death—this Wonderland. If we search persistently and are lucky enough to stumble upon our rabbit hole, we may discover our own Wonderland right under our noses, where it has always been.

One

DOWN IN A HOLE

"Have you guessed the riddle yet?" the Hatter said, turning
to Alice again.

"No, I give it up," Alice replied. "What's the answer?"

"I haven't the slightest idea," said the Hatter.

"Nor I," said the March Hare.

*W*hen my son Alex was about ten years old, he was very interested
in the concept of "being right." It was spring and we were taking a walk.
I started to tell him the names of the flowers. "This is a Red-Bearded
Snake, and that is a Blue Mongoose." Eventually, he looked up at me
and said, "You're making this up." I said, "No, I'm not." And he said,
"Yes, you are." From that point onward, our conversations have been
like playing very competitive Ping-Pong. These days we might have a
discussion about which type of computer is best. For a couple of minutes
Alex will say, "I think Macs are better," and I'll say, "Well, I don't see
it that way." He'll say yes and I'll say no. Yes no, yes no, yes no. Then
we switch, just to make the other one wrong. He'll say no, and I'll say
yes. Now Alex is twenty-nine and I'm fifty-nine, and we still poke fun

at our opinions in exactly the same way.

This "yes no, yes no" is the essence of what goes on in *Alice in Wonderland*. In Alice's above-ground life, the rules are clear and everything has its proper place. At the beginning of the story, she is sitting on a riverbank with her sister, considering making a daisy chain. It's a perfectly normal day. Then she sees a white rabbit with a watch, she follows him, and soon she falls down a hole. A big hole.

After she falls, nothing she knew above ground makes sense anymore. None of the rules are the same. She wanders around getting bigger and then smaller. She meets all kinds of characters who don't seem to be following rules at all, which causes quite a problem. They don't comply with her expectations or her understanding. They don't do anything she thinks is proper or right.

In time, Alice goes to the Mad Hatter's tea party. Alice finds the Mad Hatter and his friends, the March Hare and the Dormouse, sitting at a long table under a tree. Mysteriously, they're all cramped together on one side of the table. Alice asks if she can sit down.

> "No room! No room!" they cried out when they saw Alice coming.
> "There's plenty of room!" said Alice indignantly, and she sat down
>   in a large armchair at one end of the table.
> "Have some wine," the March Hare said in an encouraging tone.

Alice looked around the table, but there was nothing on it but tea.

> "I don't see any wine," she remarked.
> "There isn't any," said the March Hare.

"Then it wasn't very civil of you to offer it," said Alice angrily.

"It wasn't very civil of you to sit down without being invited,"
said the March Hare.

Alice has her ideas of how things should be. The March Hare, the Mad Hatter, and the Dormouse see things completely differently. According to them, there really is no room at the table. According to Alice, there is plenty of room. In this same way, we come into our life and our practice with our own ideas of how it has to be. We erect the walls of our house and block the view of the sky.

Does Alice know what the Mad Hatter is talking about? How often are we willing to accept that we don't know the answer to something? We'd rather know and be right than live in a state of wonder and uncertainty.

When we get to the other shore, to what I am calling Wonderland, we experience One Mind. One Mind is what we experience when we remove everything we know. The last thing to fall away is the idea of our separation from the world. Once that idea is gone, there is nothing left, and then you are on the other shore, in Wonderland, and experiencing One Mind. We can call it many things, but they are all ways to describe something we experience for ourselves when our thoughts become quiet and our minds concentrated for long enough.

"Do you mean that you think you can find out the answer to it?"
said the March Hare.

"Exactly so," said Alice.

"Then you should say what you mean," the March Hare went on.

"I do," Alice hastily replied; "at least—at least I mean what I say—
that's the same thing, you know."

"Not the same thing a bit!" said the Hatter. "Why, you might just as
well say that 'I see what I eat' is the same as 'I eat what I see'!"

"You might as well say," added the March Hare, "that 'I like what I
get' is the same thing as 'I get what I like'!"

Zen practice is the practice of liking what you get. We usually have a thin margin of acceptance; we like very little of what we get. We want something else. Maybe we want what we think we deserve or what we think everyone else has. We're convinced, along with Alice, that if everybody would just change his or her behavior, everything would be great. If only we lived somewhere else, if only we were younger, older, smarter, dumber, rounder, thinner, or sexier—if only all of that were true, life would be good.

We're told we're supposed to go to a particular school, work at this kind of job, marry that person; this is the yellow brick road that leads to happiness. The only problem is: no one seems happy. Somehow the original plan, which was to understand exactly where you're going and what you're doing, isn't working. We're all stuck complaining that Wonderland isn't what we think it ought to be.

This same thing has happened to me. One experience I had early in my Zen practice still makes me laugh. It was 1980 and I was a student at Zen Mountain Monastery in upstate New York. Taizan Maezumi Roshi was abbot and the resident teacher was John Daido Loori—now Roshi. The monastery was relatively new and I was the head of administration as well as a senior student. My job was to keep everything running smoothly and ensure that the monastery flourished. I felt I was doing something noble and perhaps I was; however, I was also becoming righteous, irritable, and intolerant. One day Daido was walking though the monastery office where I was working. He sat down and I unloaded all my troubles and my complaints about the staff: this one was doing that, and that one wasn't doing this.

Daido asked if I remembered the first line of the verse we chanted each evening—the Four Vows.

"Yes," I said. "Sentient beings are numberless, I vow to save them."

He said, "That's right. Now which sentient beings did you have in mind?" And he chuckled as he watched my face.

Imagine what would happen if we gave up our ideas about how everything should be. What if we could peel away our constructed reality until we come to a place where a tree is just a tree, and not our idea of what a tree should be? "Tree" is just a word. "We're walking in a field" is just an idea. But the idea of "walking in a field" also has a lot of connotations—it could suggest I won't be able to walk someday. It could suggest life and death. Our words and ideas can be full of fear. Why don't we peel those away while we're at it?

How do we get to "One Mind"? Like Alice, our lives have us bumping into saints and sages who are pointing the way, if only we could see them.

When we engage in practices—sitting and walking meditation, and mindfulness in our daily lives—we gradually create an opening from which to see the events that occur. We add some breathing space—you might call it a hole—a place a white rabbit could pop out of. Practices create possibility. What appeared to be positive or negative experiences with people or events become opportunities for practice and the growth of understanding. We can learn to welcome our experience of our lives.

We often use our fears to maintain the illusion of safety. But that kind of safety closes down our lives. Here's a tool for getting closer to Wonderland: Take a few moments to sit and breathe. Notice how often in a day you feel afraid or anxious. It may be helpful to keep a notebook and write down each time you experience this fear. Each time it comes up, stop, sit, breathe, and notice.

It can be surprising to become aware of one's fears. It takes awareness and courage to open our eyes and say, "I really don't know what's going on. Bring on the awe. Bring on the eternal. Bring on that which I don't know." When we are open to the confusion and the craziness, we get little slivers of recognition.

> ...[S]aid the Hatter with a sigh: "it's always teatime, and we've no time to wash the things between whiles."
> "Then you keep moving round, I suppose?" said Alice.
> "Exactly so," said the Hatter, "as the things get used up."

That's why there's no room for Alice at the table. They have a way of looking at things, and it works just as well as Alice's. It's always six o'clock; therefore, it's always teatime. They sit at the table and never put away the tea things. They just keep moving to a new seat and another tea set; a new seat and another tea set; a new seat and another tea set.

This is not so different from the way many of us handle our relationships. In the beginning of my relationship with my wife, Caryn, I expected it to be like other relationships I'd had. Caryn is a quiet person and somehow that seemed like a problem to me. I wanted more interaction. At one point while on a long relatively silent trip in a car, I got frustrated and she pointed out to me that quiet was her way. She asked me in a kindly way if I could just accept that. Finally, in that moment, I could. In the twenty-seven years since, the beauty of her quiet has supported our lives and practice. I was able to see the magic that is Caryn instead of the preconceptions, resistance, and habitual patterns I was bringing to our relationship. This event has been like a bookmark in my life with her. I often return to it. It is also a practice, an ongoing way of developing my appreciation for our relationship and my relationship to others.

We are alive today. A good number of us don't have to worry about where our next meal is coming from; and the weather is beautiful. If we can get a few things out of our way, then every day can be a good day; even a day when something bad happens. If we can really see this wonderful, mixed-up life that we get to be in, with all of the suffering and pleasure, then we can accept that we are in Wonderland, and even possibly enjoy the trip.

Most of us are like Alice, trying to get others to make sense (by our definition) and to do things that make us happy. Yet they won't. I know I need to remind myself of this daily: *The point of everybody else's life is not to make me happy.* What would your relationships be like if you accepted the people around you exactly as they are? There is nothing as transformative as being okay with everything. The craving to transform, to change, to make rules, to push people into shapes we like, isn't effective. It doesn't make us feel closer with our friends and family. Instead of trying to change others, maybe we can accept them as they are. Maybe we can even try to make *them* happy. They'd like that, since they likely think the point of everybody else's life is to make them happy!

When Alice wants to have a normal conversation with the Dormouse, she's quite sure it's time to start making sense.

> "Once upon a time there were three little sisters," the Dormouse
> began, in a great hurry; "and their names were Elsie, Lacie, and
> Tillie; and they lived at the bottom of a well—"
> "What did they live on?" asked Alice, who always took a great
> interest in questions of eating and drinking.
> "They lived on treacle," said the Dormouse, after thinking a minute
> or two.
> "They couldn't have done that, you know," Alice gently remarked.
> "They'd have been ill."
> "So they were," said the Dormouse, "very ill."
> "But they were in the well," Alice said to the Dormouse, not
> choosing to notice his last remark.
> "Of course they were," said the Dormouse, "well in."
> This answer so confused poor Alice that she let the Dormouse go

on for some time without interrupting it.

"They were learning to draw," the Dormouse went on, yawning and rubbing its eyes, for it was getting very sleepy, "and they drew all manner of things—everything that begins with an M—"

"Why with an M?" said Alice.

"Why not?" said the March Hare.

Koans are a device used in Zen training. They are questions that need to be answered experientially, using insight, not intellect. They are usually drawn from the record of conversations between the old Zen masters and their students. The word *koan* translates roughly as "public case," like a law. It refers to something about which there is a level of common understanding.

Koans are questions that provide an opportunity to leave the intellect behind. They are like chances to fly. When done with the right spirit, they provide a practice of forgetting the intellectual construct of self and joining the larger self the koan is pointing at. In time, life can become a koan practice in which we can learn to abandon our point of view and accept people and events that we might have resisted due to our conditioning, our story. Although koans are presented in many types of dialogues or poetic phrases, the heart of all koans is one question. What is the self? Who are you? Each koan is an opportunity to wake up to Wonderland.

In my own training, I've practiced with about seven hundred koans over a period of twenty-five years. Often there were additional challenges involved besides "seeing" the koan. We did koan practice in a tiny room called the *dokusan* room. Very early in the morning an assistant would announce dokusan and everyone would run from the meditation hall to the dokusan line, elbowing and pushing for the privilege of getting in line, and hopefully, into the dokusan room for a one-on-one meeting with a teacher. The practice was even more challenging when Maezumi Roshi was in the dokusan room. I would finally make it through the line and into the room only to hear Maezumi Roshi whisper, in his strong Japanese accent, words I could not decipher. I had to ask him to repeat himself over and over again. Outside the window, birds were singing, insects buzzing, water burbling. All these sounds mingled with Roshi and my koan. It was disorienting and magical. Perhaps Alice felt something similar on her way down the hole.

One of the koans asks the question, "The world is vast and wide. Why do we put on the seven-paneled robe (a traditional monk's robe) at the sound of a bell?"

This question could be translated as: *We are free. Why do we tie ourselves up?* But looking more deeply, the question might lead us to more questions. There are so many ways in which we're used to thinking about things, and so much we take for granted when we use language. The purpose of a koan is to wake us up from taking language—and the world around us—for granted.

What is the meaning of rain? Why do we walk in the woods? In Buddhism, we cultivate something called aimlessness, which means being and acting for the sole purpose of being or acting in that way, without a further goal, motive, or ambition. We put on the robe to put on the robe. We love simply to love.

The Dormouse had closed its eyes by this time, and was going off into a doze; but, on being pinched by the Hatter, it woke up again with a little shriek, and went on: "—that begins with an M, such as mousetraps, and the moon, and memory, and muchness—you know you say things are 'much of a muchness'—did you ever see such a thing as a drawing of a muchness?"

"Really, now that you ask me," said Alice, very much confused, "I don't think—"

Muchness could be another word for a term we use in Buddhism: *suchness*. It means "things as they are," thus, before conceptual thought intrudes, separates, judges, and elaborates. For example, we see the white snow and we think we are seeing just snow, the "suchness" of the snow. But by naming it and putting it in the category "snow," where we already have a preconceived notion of what snow is, we are putting a filter over the thing itself, separating us from fully experiencing its "suchness."

Mind creates all separation. Yet even the thing we call mind is just a word for what can't be grasped or put into a category of existence or nonexistence, large or small, collective or individual. Therefore, anybody's stupidity is just as good as anybody else's. Anybody's completely constructed view of reality is just as good as anybody else's—with one exception. If we create a reality that hurts other people, puts them on the outside, or makes them feel pain in any form, that view of reality creates an effect. That is what separates one reality from another: each perception bringing about a different consequence.

This is what is meant by *karma*. Karma is often explained either too magically or too simplistically. I like to think of it as simple cause and effect. Cause and effect isn't something unique to individuals. A country, a time period, or an idea can all create cause and effect. In our own life we can clearly see that our actions toward others have a lot to do with what we get back from them. Showing sensitivity and kindness to others will not only please them, it will also transform us. The minute we stop believing that everything unpleasant that happens to us is someone else's fault, everything will change.

When I was a kid, I used to bounce a ball and chant: *A, my name is Alice and my husband's name is Abraham and we live in Alaska and we sell apples. B, my name is Barbara and my husband's name is Bob and we live in Bovina and we sell bubbles.* This children's game is a rehearsal for joining mainstream American society. We label ourselves: I am a doctor, a lawyer, a computer programmer, a mother, a father. What if none of that is who we really are? What if we were to get up in the morning without any preconceived notions of who we are?

We say in our practice that to realize the *dharma* is to forget the self. Dharma is a word that means "the teaching," or "the truth." It has different nuances of meaning in different contexts. We have a lineage, going all the way back to fifth century China, of incredible teachers who would deliberately do to students what the Mad Hatter and his friends are doing to Alice—knock her out of her thinking mind. When you ask people to recall a time when they were happy, they often describe a time of being with friends, or hiking in nature, or swimming in the ocean, a time when they were in a state of mind beyond thinking.

In the movie *Serpico*, a New York City policeman meets a young woman and asks, "What are you?" She answers, "I'm an actress, a dancer, a writer, and a Buddhist." *B my name is Bob and I'm a Buddhist*. Don't be a Buddhist. If you're sure you're a Buddhist, then you're not looking at what you might be in that moment. When Bodhidharma was asked who he was by the emperor of China, he answered, "I don't know." Bodhidharma is the legendary figure who brought Buddhism from India to China. It is said he lived to be 110 years old. He is known for meditating in a cave for many years. He was very brave and very truthful. He didn't just tell the truth; he sang it like a great soaring eagle.

Buddhism is not going to make us a Buddha. Nobody is going to make us a Buddha. We're already a Buddha. Buddha just means someone who is awakened. What do we have to do to be awakened? Wake up to the present moment.

Waking up to the present moment means stopping the relentless chatter of our associative minds. The sad part is that most of the chatter isn't very pleasant anyway; the chatter in our mind is often about fear, blame, anger, and all those wonderful things. The practice of stopping thoughts is one I often ask students to work on. I remember the first time I discovered I could do that. What a sense of freedom to realize that when I didn't know what to do, when I didn't know the answer, I could simply stop. I could wake up. This experience was key to me wanting to practice.

But it's hard to wake up when we have all these ideas. We need a reminder, a gentle shove. When we walk outside, the trees and the sun can be reminders to stop and wake up. If it snows, if the wind blows, these are also reminders. If there is someone in the house when you come home, and they smile at you, that is also a lovely reminder. We can begin to appreciate all the gifts that are pouring into our eyes and ears and that surround us at every moment.

I met my wife Caryn at Zen Mountain Monastery over thirty years ago. Eventually we moved into a place called Esopus House, which was deep in the country. The Northeast winters were very cold and Esopus House was small and drafty. The little woodstove didn't even keep the place heated through the night. Early every morning we would walk down the road for morning meditation. Across the road was the Esopus—the stream the house was named for. One particular morning, we opened the sliding doors to an incredible roar of water. Spring had come and the Esopus was surging free in the darkness of the morning. There was nothing in the world for us but that stream. Caryn and I looked at each other in awe; not here, there, or anywhere. We were out of our minds with wonder.

Suppose we are able to touch this Wonderland for a moment. Then we are, like Alice, brought back to the familiar world. What can we do? Let's say we have a moment when we're not resisting anything anymore. What are we going to do? Well, many of us then try to hold on to the One Mind. We might begin to tell others about it, try to persuade them of its truth. We might encourage them toward a seminar or a meditation class.

If we do any of that, we've lost Wonderland again. If we start thinking, "I know what's happening. I'm a Buddhist," we're grasping too tightly. The only way to hold on to the wonder of the moment is to let it go.

We all feel we're in our particular lives without having chosen them. To consciously choose our human existence is a profound and beautiful practice. To be in touch with the wonder, we have to truly be wherever we find ourselves. The place of wonder can never be different from the place we're in.

The wonder of life is what we experience every day—washing our hands, breathing, taking a walk, working. There is no place to go other than here. Can we throw ourselves into that fully without understanding it? Do we have to know why we put on the seven-paneled robe?

When I was five or six and we were living in Danville, Illinois, my mother took me with her to visit a friend. She sat me down in a garden while she and her friend talked. I sat there for what seemed like an eternity looking around in wonder. I couldn't believe the colors and shapes; I looked inside the flowers and the colors changed. I was enthralled. That experience is still there when I allow it. It's there in the red rocks, in the sage, in my wife's face. The practice of restoring wonder, restoring awe, is the practice of Zen.

Two

NEZ

*L*enny Bruce, the famous comic, was truthful and outspoken. He got into trouble because he used unacceptable language to get deep into people's manure. If Zen practice is going to reach you, go right down in the hole with it and be willing to be thrown out of everything familiar. Lenny Bruce used to talk about people having "Nez." Nez is the opposite of Zen. Nez is the feeling that something is not as it should be. Many of us spend every minute of our lives in Nez. We think, "If I could just change this one thing, then everything would be great. I'd be enlightened." Nez is like the constant refrain, "if only." If only this would change, if only that person would change, if only people would understand me, if only, if only, if only. The Mock Turtle sings "The Lobster Quadrille":

> Would not, could not, would not, could not, would not join the
> dance.
> Would not, could not, would not, could not, could not join the
> dance.

Let's say you're studying with a teacher, and he's annoying you. He insists that you make a change—the very thing you came in here for, but of course, you think he's asking you to make exactly the wrong change. Usually the change is to stop blaming other people. Don't be angry, don't be afraid, don't think that life is going to get better when you move to California—although it might. You say to yourself, "If only he'd stop harping on that thing and help me get enlightened." That's Nez.

> "Would you tell me, please, which way I ought to go from here?"
> "That depends a good deal on where you want to get to," said the Cat.
> "I don't much care where—" said Alice.
> "Then it doesn't matter which way you go," said the Cat.

A benefit of training—whether in sports, music, or anything else— is that the training process is generally less about opinions and more about practice. You focus on learning to run or swim or play music at a certain level. You look into the reasons you might not be making enough progress in your training only because this can help you improve your practice.

I once worked as a studio musician. I liked studio work because it paid well, but you had to perform under pressure, the same as an athlete. If you missed a take on your instrument and had to do it over, it would cost the producer $500. Enough takes and soon you'd be out of work.

Zen practice is not static. If we've been practicing for twenty-five or thirty years, we understand that our practice should reveal itself in some way, and that we shouldn't just sit there, year after year, with nothing changing. There is a koan that can help us relate to what our responsibility in our life of practice really is:

> An old master, Hoen of Tozan, said, "Shakyamuni and
> Maitreya are his servants; now tell me, who is he?"

Shakyamuni is the historical Buddha, a realized one of the past, and Maitreya is the realized one of the future. It's important not to push this away as something that doesn't concern *us*. Words like "Buddha" and phrases like "realized one" can make what we're hearing or reading seem distant, exotic, beyond our capacity. That's what this koan is talking about. Have you guessed who he (or she) is? Yes, it's *you*.

The koan points to the deepest parts of the self, the ocean of self. There is a poem from a thirteenth-century collection of koans called the *Mumonkan*, or *The Gateless Gate*.

> Do not draw another person's bow;
> Do not ride another person's horse;
> Do not defend another person's faults;
> Do not inquire into another person's affairs.

So when does a sense of responsibility, the desire to embody, to be the practice, happen in Zen? As soon as you "practice for the joy of practicing," you can feel it right away. If that freedom doesn't show— the freedom that comes from knowing you are the only one who can bind yourself and that your restrictions and suffering are nobody else's fault—then you're not practicing. Maybe you like sitting cross-legged in meditation; maybe you like incense; maybe you think if you feel pain, something is happening. You're contemplating practicing instead of practicing. Dogen Zenji says in a famous fascicle of his twelfth-century masterwork, the Shobogenzo:

> To study the Buddha Way is to study the self,
> To study the self is to forget the self,
> To forget the self is to be enlightened by the ten thousand things.
> This means we can be enlightened by anything and everything.

The first part of this quote, "to study the self," is important. It means you need to see what you do. If you are part of a Zen sitting group, eventually you can't help but see what you do. That's truly Zen practice. It's not practice if you just sit every morning and then blame somebody else, or walk away the moment a problem comes up in your life. To pretend these frustrations have nothing to do with your practice is to avoid the study of the self. We can focus too much on our realization and avoid the serious attempt to get down and dirty with the self, *your* self. This is mud wrestling and you are the mud. I am the mud, too. We're all here in the mud of our jealousies, our angers, and our fears. Enlightenment is not something separate, but is rooted in our awareness of these things.

Many of our behaviors, emotional reactions, and ways of thinking are mechanical, not conscious. They're deeply ingrained habits and they create suffering, not just for others, but for ourselves. This is also where the teacher is very important. Some of us like to do Zen practice. A lot of us probably don't. But as I said, there's simply nothing better to do.

"Devotion" is the word I was taught. What does it mean to be devoted? Most of us have a rough idea. It brings me back to hearing the Everly Brothers singing "Devoted to You" when I was sixteen years old. My friends and I were hanging out on a street corner, leaning into the open window of a parked car, listening to the music coming out of the car's radio, anxious to hear the new music, the new message. Their idea of devotion was clearly about romance:

> Through the years our love will grow.
> Like a river it will flow.
> Until then I'll always be
> devoted to you.

Many times when we're young, we may bond with someone, get into a relationship, or get married even though it's not clear what we're devoted to. We enjoy the sexual chemistry and romance. This is natural and the world needs it. We're like flowers, the world needs us to bloom. But what can we truly be devoted to?

Devoted means "one with." You can be devoted to your life and your death. Every moment of your life is nothing other than enlightenment. There is no other teaching outside the moment to moment of your very life. To be devoted to that—to practice it, realize it, and appreciate it— is the dharma, the teaching. Appreciating every moment of your life does not mean living only for the moment; it's not about grabbing the moment and wringing the most pleasure you can out of it. To appreci- ate every instant of your life requires maintaining a constant awareness of life and death.

One of the basic tenets of Buddhism is that life is suffering. We age, we get sick, and we die. We lose those we love. Many of us have a problem relating to the idea that life is suffering because we're having such a good time, especially if we're young and we think we're immortal and not just passing through, and especially if we're privileged and live in an affluent society. But even our transitory thoughts—*I wish it were hotter, I wish it were colder, I wish this person didn't treat me this way, I wish the soup wasn't so salty, I wish I didn't live in Utah*—create pain and suffering. The Buddha's true Dharma body, our true body, is the empty sky that responds to things as forms appear. Think of the moon. The moon doesn't know it's a moon. The moon is full and its light shines everywhere. Your life doesn't know it's your life. For you there is nothing outside your life and every moment of your life is your full life. It's a light that shines everywhere. There's no place your life doesn't touch. Your life is made up of everything that isn't your life, including the moon, the flowers, and other people.

Without effort, the moon manifests differently according to circumstances. The moon appears large when it's reflected in a lake and small when it's reflected in a drop of rain. Enlightenment adapts to the circumstances in which it finds itself. Even though your life is part of everything throughout eternity, it manifests at a particular time according to circumstances. Right now, your life is manifesting as you read this book. This is cause and effect. When you stop reading, your life will still continue according to karma. We are the center of our universe. We don't see our own karma completely, but it's still our own. Nobody is stopping us from living our enlightened mind to its fullest. That is being one with our karma as it manifests right here, right now.

Dogen Zenji is considered by many to be the most important teacher in the Soto school of Zen. His writings are profound and beautiful. Here is an excerpt from "Tsuki," or "The Moon," a fascicle from the Shobogenzo.

> Thusness, is the moon in water. It is water thusness, moon
> thusness, thusness within, within thusness. "Thus" does
> not mean "like something." "Thus" means "as it is."

This is so direct and elegant. "Thus" doesn't mean "like this." It doesn't mean "like that." At this moment, your life is "thus." To think in terms of "like this" or "like that" is to step away from this very moment, which is our life. Master Dogen describes this as losing our lives.

My teacher, Genpo Roshi, has a muscular devotion to Zen practice. Daido Roshi also threw his whole being into the practice. The two of them trained together. They often shared a room during intensive Zen retreats, or *sesshin*. Sesshin is a Japanese word that means "to settle the mind." The character *shin* is both mind and heart, so it can also be understood as "settling the heart." Daido Roshi used to call Genpo Roshi a Zen jock because when everyone got up at 4:30 in the morning to sit, Genpo Roshi would already have been sitting for an hour. That's devotion. Devotion is a practice and an emotional commitment.

Maezumi Roshi was a complex man: strong, yet soft and sensitive. He had absolutely no shame; he would beg you to practice. Then, if you practiced, he would thank you repeatedly. On one weeklong visit, he thanked me at least fifty times. And then he said, "I want you to become a monk. Please become a monk. Please don't waste your life. Please don't let down this beautiful dharma. Please devote yourself to this dharma."

That devotion has kept our lineage alive. The old Zen masters were devoted to getting all of us to realize our life as it is, right here, right now, to realize the mind that is beyond life and death. Isn't that valuable? There's a mind in which there is *no* life and death, and there's a mind in which there *is* life and death. The mind in which there is life and death is a mind filled with concepts. Your true mind does not have concepts. It doesn't think, "I'm going to live," or "I'm going to die." Your real mind is just "thus." You walk your dog, you look at a tree, and you enjoy your life. Each moment of life, exactly as it is lived, is what it means to practice the dharma. If you don't appreciate your life, it's not anybody's fault. It's not even your fault. Enjoying your life takes practice.

Transactional analysis, or TA, was a popular form of therapy in the 1970s. There is a Zen angle to TA, a progression which takes us from the usual, dualistic way we see ourselves and others, to having a larger, more inclusive view. The progression starts with: *I'm not OK but you're OK* or, *You're not OK but I'm OK*. Next we move to the transactional idea: *I'm OK and you're OK*. I like to think there's another level: *I'm not OK and you're not OK, and that's OK.*

There is a Buddhist chant, the morning *gatha*, which says, "All greed, anger, and ignorance born of my body, mouth, and thought...." This refers to everyone who unconsciously walks around angry, greedy, and ignorant, making others unhappy in the process. We all have greed and ignorance. If we'd like to change it, then let's go, let's work on it. Everything that matters requires devotion, and everybody in your life needs it: your partner, friends, family, and society. All beings need your devotion.

When I saw that devotion was missing from my life, I realized it wasn't just missing from my Zen practice; it was missing from all aspects of my life. I wasn't truly being with the things in my life. I wasn't truly appreciating them. When I was reading a book, I was restless. When I was talking to a friend, I was thinking about the next thing I had to do. I was doing everything with "one hand." We live in a disposable culture. We get something, we use it, and when we're done with it, we throw it away—whether it's a hammer, a friend, or our partner. We aren't ex-pected to devote ourselves to anything, so we don't practice being loyal or committing ourselves to things or to people.

In the book *Reframing* by Richard Bandler and John Grinder, there's a story about a woman who visited a therapist because she was angry with her husband and son. They never picked up after themselves, they didn't care about their surroundings, and the house looked like a garbage dump. Her therapist advised her to go home, wait until they were away, and then clean up the whole house. He told her to make it just the way she liked it, and once the house was perfect, to sit and contemplate it. So she cleaned the house, she sat down, and immediately she burst into tears. At her next session, the therapist asked her what had made her cry. She said, "Because the clean house meant that my husband and son were gone."

You'll never make your life perfect if you're still living it. Life comes with a lot of shit but it can be "good shit." My favorite jazz teacher used to refer to good music as good shit. Can we appreciate the good manure? Manure is perfect, but not in the way we tend to conceive of perfection.

During part of the time I was studying with Genpo Roshi, I felt that all the senior students were competitive and insensitive. I had a good excuse for my own "faultlessness"; I was recovering from Guillain-Barré syndrome, a neurological disorder that causes paralysis. I was seeing a lot of Genpo Roshi and doing a lot of complaining. One day we went to the gym together and I was telling him about the competitiveness of the students. He started to chuckle and asked if I had noticed that I was competitive, too. It was the last thing I expected to hear and the first I needed to. Genpo Roshi helped me acknowledge and accept my own competitive traits. He helped me understand that although these traits might exist in myself and in others, not to judge or complain, but to do my best.

Whenever I get stuck in this kind of blaming, whenever I think I have all the answers, whenever I take the higher moral ground, I eventually regret it and realize that I need to examine and accept some part of myself.

Will you, won't you, will you, won't you, will you join the dance?
Will you, won't you, will you, won't you, won't you join the dance?

The option is to take on whatever we get as we dance, right here where we are, and not to go out chasing "if onlys." We realize that it's better "here" when I'm really "here," and it's better "there" when I'm really "there." That's the beauty of this radical dharma; it puts us right where we are and we don't know where that is. The practice starts where concepts stop. Then you're in Wonderland. Otherwise, it's Nez.

Master Dogen talks about "timeless spring." What a beautiful phrase. Timeless spring is the spring of no season. Timeless spring is summer when you're one with summer, autumn when you're one with autumn, winter when you're one with winter, and spring when you're one with spring.

My wife and I were watching a friend play guitar. He was deeply into the music. There is a certain way of playing jazz, in which you lean into the instrument and even talk to yourself while you play. Talking to yourself, singing the improvs, and playing the instrument with your whole body, is a jazz tradition. That's what our friend was doing, and I was thinking, Yes, that's how you have to practice. You have to get down into it and really put your soul into it, unafraid of the mud. Only your ego can stop you.

This doesn't mean you have to pretend to feel something you don't feel. Practicing Zen—sitting with your feelings, sitting and breathing with the present moment—can be difficult and confusing when we first approach it. In the beginning, I never trusted any of my teachers. Then one day I woke up and said, Oh, my god. I've been doing this practice with these wonderful teachers. I thought they were abusing me but they were teaching me. Suddenly, I understood what they were trying to tell me about myself and the dharma. I was tying myself up in knots and they were trying to set me free. Dogen says:

> Buddha's true Dharma body is the "as it is" of empty sky.
> This empty sky is the "as it is" of Buddha's true Dharma
> body. Because it is Buddha's true Dharma body, the entire
> Earth, the entire universe, all phenomena, and all ap-
> pearances are empty sky. Hundreds of grasses and myriad
> forms—each appearing "as it is"—are nothing but Bud-
> dha's true Dharma body, thusness of the moon in water.

What he's saying is that when we drop our concepts and ideas, the silent mind contains everything. That's our true body. Stop thinking, and you're in the One Mind. It has no edges, no limits, no beginning, and no ending. That is the body we had before our mothers and fathers were born. That body does not come into existence, it does not go out of existence, it cannot be understood, and it cannot be grasped. This is your true body; and it is the body of the Buddha. What is it worth to realize who you really are and that there's nothing to be afraid of? Most of the things we fret over in our daily life turn out to be small matters. All the worries, all the anxieties, all the suffering are caused by your mind running in circles. For 2,500 years, our lineage has, through sweat, blood, death, and sheer determination, kept this one message alive so we could hear it: We are the enlightened body. Can you be your enlightened body? Can you be the moon that doesn't know itself but that still shines everywhere?

You might be thinking, "What's so hot about not knowing? What has it ever gotten me?" I know you need to function in the world. I'm not asking you to stop thinking or to give up knowing things. Just ask yourself, "How important is knowing the periodic table of elements compared to knowing who you are, what your life is about, where you're going, or where you came from?" Not so important, right? In the meantime, it's nice to know the table of elements, too. We are beginning to find out that having knowledge about how our planet works is very important. One doesn't negate the other.

To devote oneself body and soul to experiencing one's life and death is to live the life of a Buddha. Devotion means not backing away from obstacles. Devotion is throwing oneself into something completely. In contrast, hopping around like your feet are on fire is normal life. You're moving from spot to spot hoping that someday things will cool off. They won't. Years go by and the flame manifests as anger, irritation, or the nonacceptance of people. This fire is common in relationships. We think the other person starts the fire; they're the pyromaniac, not us. If you love somebody and you stop thinking about how they should be different, you'll probably wind up loving them more. That's what love is, letting them be. If somebody is your project, let that project go. Get some LEGOs instead.

If your feet are on fire and you sit still, the fire will eventually put itself out. We call this process *zazen* meditation. When you're on fire, just sit still. After a while, there will be less air to feed the fire. If you sit there long enough, the bonfire will eventually become smaller. It's not so bad now. People are no longer running out of the room when you come in; they're just slowly walking out.

Sit some more. Now the fire is just a warm ember. People still feel like leaving when you walk in the room, but they're too lazy to get up.

The fire isn't so troublesome. It's not burning hot enough to hurt someone; your toes aren't emitting flames, they're just glowing a little.

There's a koan in which a teacher is interviewing a prospective student and asks where he's been. The student gives an innocent answer and the teacher hits him and throws him out. The student lies awake all night tormented by thoughts of right and wrong. "What did I do and why did he do that? What could I have done differently? Is he just a jerk? Are we both crazy? What am I doing?" The next morning, the student comes into the *zendo*, makes his bows, and asks, "Where was my fault?" Wouldn't we like the people closest to us in our lives to ask, "Where was my fault?" rather than blaming us?

We teach each other, we are each other, we see our inner Buddha reflected in each other. Practicing and listening: that is devotion manifested. Training over and over is devotion. The rest will just happen. The moon rises every night and makes no effort to cast its reflection on the water.

Three

CASTING OFF

The Diamond Sutra is a scripture in the Mahayana Buddhist canon. We can think of it as a discourse. It is very old, probably going back to just after the start of the Common Era. Yet for me it is also brand new, and it cuts through my thinking each time I read it. I remember first reading the words "This world is not a world, therefore it is provisionally called a world." It shook me. It made me realize how much I had let words and concepts govern and limit me. The Diamond Sutra questions our concepts of self and cuts through everything we've fixed and made immovable in our thoughts.

> Thus shall ye think of this fleeting world:
> A star at dawn, a bubble in a stream;
> a flash of lightning in a summer cloud,
> a flickering lamp, a phantom and a dream.

These lines lift all the anchors—they let us cast off.

My wife Caryn and I once visited Puerto Escondido in Mexico. Although Caryn is afraid of deep water, I wanted to sail, so I rented a small sailboat and took it out alone. Caryn read a book on the beach, and she waved as I left. I had learned to sail in high school. I went to an all-boys high school. Once in awhile my friends and I would skip school, rent a sailboat at City Island and sail to Brighton Beach. It was a really cool thing to do and always impressed the young girls. So when Caryn and I went to Mexico I was excited; I thought maybe I'd just sail right off to South America! I was sailing and the land was disappearing; I was thinking that if I kept sailing in this direction, I'd hit Peru, when suddenly I realized that I'd never sailed a boat by myself before. It hadn't occurred to me that every time I'd been in a boat, there had been at least one other person to whom I could hand a line.

The realization that I had no one to hand a line to came back to me recently. When I left the East Coast for Utah in 1997, I was accompanied by a small group of fellow practitioners. Except for my friends Jules and Cathy, they have all since moved away. I am at a great physical distance from everyone who was part of my life before I turned fifty and I'm not in touch very often with many people from my past. In the desert, I felt I was becoming as unmoored as I had been in that boat.

I drove up to the hills surrounding Mill Creek Canyon to think. Sitting above the Canyon, where it's quiet, I thought about everything changing. When I came down, I went over to the house my friends lived in. There was a big moving truck in the driveway and on the back of the truck was the company's logo, a sailboat.

The Diamond Sutra says:

All the Bodhisattva Heroes should discipline their thoughts
as follows: All living creatures of whatever class, born from
eggs, from wombs, from moisture, or by transformation,
whether with form or without form, whether in a state
of thinking or exempt from thought-necessity, or wholly
beyond all thought realms—all these are caused by me to
attain Unbounded Liberation Nirvana. Why is this? It is
because no bodhisattva who is a real bodhisattva cherishes
the idea of an ego entity, a personality, a being, or a sepa-
rated individuality.

Realization is what leads us to liberation. The Buddha says, "All beings
are led by me." That also means by you. We are all led by our awakened
mind. These qualities are already inside us and can lead us to realize
them more fully. It's our Buddha nature that realizes Buddha. The ego
can only grasp the ego. A buddha understands the self as something
beyond personality, beyond being, with no separate individuality.

The idea that we're a self and that we're lost is just another thought.
Thinking, "Okay, I get it. I'm a self and that's the whole problem,"
creates another problem. The mystery of our existence and how to live
the best life is not solved by thought. The Buddha uses the words *do not
cherish an idea*. Saying, "Okay, I'm going to sit in non-striving mind,"
is not it. Saying, "Okay, I'm going to go deeper," is not it. Thought is
solved by no-thought, the backward step.

The only position that allows us to experience a buddha's liberation is no position. Even to take the position of forgetting the self—in other words, to not have an ego—is still a position. Any position is a wrong position. Buddha is coming from no position. No thought, no self, no non-self either. There's nothing wrong with having an ego, our ego is part of us. The problem is how much power we let it have over us. Our ego tells us it's our true self, our only self, it limits, it binds, it takes our freedom. It doesn't allow us to fully live in this magical world. It doesn't let us fly. Down in the hole Alice could no longer ground herself in her ego.

> The Caterpillar was the first to speak.
> "What size do you want to be?"
> "Oh, I'm not particular as to size," Alice hastily replied; "only one doesn't like changing so often, you know."
> "I don't know," said the Caterpillar.

A person with a strong sense of self in relationship to others usually functions well. The person who has a fragile ego or tries not to have an ego is more problematic. Counter to what we might expect, the person who doesn't have to prove anything and doesn't feel the need to lord their power over anyone is more easily able to see beyond the self, is quicker to fly, and finds it easier to come home. I love Carlos Castaneda's books *Journey to Ixtlan* and *The Power of Silence.* Don Juan is a Yaqui Indian and inheritor of a tradition of knowledge who takes Carlos on a journey into the unknown. He is a great flight instructor. To enter the magical region of the unknown we need to leave the ground of knowing. This is our practice of falling through the hole of reason to the suchness of things, unencumbered by our ideas about them. A positive sense of self allows someone to be flexible and to experience new areas. This unstuck-ness, or ability to let go, eventually allows us to be free and unattached to concepts.

The Diamond Sutra says:

So you should not be attached to things as being possessed of, or devoid of, intrinsic qualities.

This is the reason why the Tathagata always teaches this saying:

My teaching of the Good Law is to be likened unto a raft. The Buddha-teaching must be relinquished; how much more so mis-teaching!

Buddha never called himself a Buddhist. Sometimes I consider myself a Buddhist and sometimes I don't. I'm thinking of alternating days! When I start to think of myself as a Buddhist, I'm tempted to wear Buddhist clothing or put a "Love Animals, Don't Eat Them" bumper sticker on my car. The Buddha simply discovered what he called "the good law," and it's not so different from the Gospel, the Good News. He found something that was self-verifying and true: we all have Buddha nature, a nature full of compassion and free of attachment to particular views and constructs. But to touch our own nature, we've got to log in some hours on the cushion. Understanding takes a lot of time, and if you're slow like I am, it takes even longer.

The description of a *kalpa* seems wonderfully appropriate. A kalpa is a measure of time. One kalpa is the time it takes to wear down Mount

Everest with an angel's wing brushing against it once every thousand years. Well, maybe finding your Buddha nature won't take you quite that long, but it sure needs more than an afternoon.

I have mentioned koans as deep questions used in Zen training. Koans are terse and elegant. Being the koan is koan study. Just being the temple bell or the rain or the sound *mu*—no separation. The word *mu* means "nothing," or "no." When his concentration is strong enough, a person becomes one with the sound mu, and then the meaning of the word is not important. The self falls away, the sound mu is the whole world—all separation falls away; the empty self includes everything.

Koan study is a way to experience the reality the Buddha is affirming. The Buddha lets go, and, as in koans, simply *is*. The Buddha went into the reality of no separation and he didn't turn back. I've had to learn how not to turn back, and I'm still learning. Maybe you are too. On that boat in Mexico, I said out loud to myself, "Coming about, back to the mainland, please." And I turned back. I'm sure the Buddha had to come about two or three times, too. He might have said, "Okay, this is the true dharma, this is how it really is." But "this is how it really is" is still a thought, it's not really how it is. Thought is not the ultimate reality. Once we cut through thought there is no dualism. After that we have to be sure we don't get stuck in the pond of nonduality, that we really are casting off, always casting off.

"You can really have no notion how delightful it will be
    When they take us up and throw us, with the lobsters, out to sea!"
    But the snail replied, "Too far, too far!" and gave a look askance—
    Said he thanked the whiting kindly, but he would not join the dance.

The Buddha says that to cast away his teaching is true faith. So how do we practice this non-cherishing, non-grasping, and non-self? We push off like a boat leaving a burning island. Don't look back, worry about it later. After we have really gotten off the island of duality, then we can turn around and take a look. But for a while, don't check, just push off.

In order to "see," sometimes we have teachers help push us off the island of duality. Master Linji used a stick to wake up students. My own teachers have used heartfelt encouragement, very long sitting meditations, and insistence on my best efforts. When you hear the shout, when you feel the slap, when the stick flies, remember that it's there to help you. There's no individuality or identity. The shout is realization of the One Mind—no thoughts or concepts attached to it, just our one original mind.

Our light shines all the time, the music is always playing. The whole world and every second of our lives is the music, but instead of being the music, we shut it down and think about it.

"Once," said the Mock Turtle at last, with a deep sigh,
"I was a real Turtle."

In the Diamond Sutra, we read the words of the Buddha:

Subhuti, what do you think? Is the Tathagata to be recognized by some material characteristic?
No, World-honored One; the Tathagata cannot be recognized by any material characteristic. Wherefore? Because the

Tathagata has said that material characteristics are not, in fact, material characteristics.

Buddha said: Subhuti, wheresoever are material characteristics there is delusion; but whosoever perceives that all characteristics are in fact no characteristics, perceives the Tathagata.

There are no characteristics. How can we see characteristics as no characteristics? When the mind doesn't move, there are no characteristics.

This theme is continued in the Prajñaparamita Heart Sutra:

No eye, ear, nose, tongue, body, mind; no color, sound, smell, taste, touch, phenomena; no realm of sight, no realm of consciousness; no ignorance and no end to ignorance; no old age and death and no end to old age and death; no suffering, no cause of suffering, no extinguishing, no path, no wisdom and no gain.

Nothing, not a particle. There isn't a thing. The bottom line is, the mind creates how we see things. If our mind doesn't move, there isn't a thing that is separate from every other thing. There also isn't *not* a thing. Reality is beyond such pairs of opposites. When the two famous Zen monks, Seppo and Ganto, were asked for their deepest teaching, one replied, "What is this?" and the other one said, "This is it."

Knowing is just a thought. Characteristics are just a thought. The world—the idea that we live in a world—is just a thought, a perception. That we have a body is just a thought, a way of seeing. What is it "to have"? What if we remove all this and start saying, "Just words, just concepts, no that's not it, just another duality, just another word, just another concept."

> Does the Buddha have a teaching to announce? Subhuti
> responds to the Buddha's question: As I understand Buddha's
> meaning there is no formulation of truth called Consumma-
> tion of Incomparable Enlightenment. Moreover, the Tathagata
> has no formulated teaching to enunciate. Wherefore? Because
> the Tathagata has said that truth is uncontainable and inex-
> pressible. It neither is nor is not.

This sounds like the Buddha to me. It's so clear. The teaching is
ungraspable; the teaching is nothing other than what's in front of us. It
neither *is* nor *is not*. You can't say it exists or doesn't exist. It can't be
compared to anything.

We have a tendency to believe we are the only ones doing things
right. When I started working as a musician, I felt everyone was either
too commercial, focused on profit, or too mainstream. I had the same
impression when I came to Zen. My critical mind was sure certain people
were not idealistic enough, or were selling out. Once someone said to
me, "You know, Daniel, you're stuck in idealism." He was right. I was
stuck in my idea of idealism. But I didn't see that. We don't see that
our particular ideas are only ideas, too. We just see that other people
are stuck in their ideas.

Buddha is saying there's no teaching to understand. There is no
"thing" that is "the right way." There is no particular reality in ideas
that you can embrace and say, "This is it." You can't get yourself around
reality; you *are* reality. You can't *get it* because you already *are* it.

There's nothing you need to do. There's no place you need to go. There's nothing to understand. What would it be like if we walked around each day not trying to understand anything? We might find that we understand much more. Groucho Marx famously said that he wouldn't want to be a member of any club that would have him as a member. But we already *are* members. In fact there is only one member and we're all that one member. Part of Siddhartha's realization that he was a buddha was that he realized everyone else was a buddha, too. The Diamond Sutra continues:

> Subhuti, this may be likened to a human frame as large
> as the mighty Mount Sumeru. What do you think? Would
> such a body be great?
> Subhuti replied: Great indeed, World-honored One. This
> is because Buddha has explained that no body is called a
> great body.
> This is the One Mind, the attainment of the Consummation
> of the Incomparable Enlightenment.
> Then Subhuti asked Buddha: World-honored One, in the
> attainment of the Consummation of Incomparable Enlight-
> enment, did Buddha make no acquisition whatsoever?
> Wait a minute. You mean the Buddha went shopping and
> came home with nothing?

Beginning our practice is like going through a revolving door into a gigantic department store. We can't wait to look at all the great stuff. We wander around and eventually we come back and stand in front of the revolving door. We're exactly where we were when we started. After all those years of practice, what's different? We have lost our desire to go through the revolving doors. We can't be in the world the same way as we used to.

> Buddha replied: Just so, Subhuti. Through the Consumma-
> tion of Incomparable Enlightenment I acquired not even
> the least thing; wherefore it is called "Consummation of
> Incomparable Enlightenment."
> Thus shall ye think of all this fleeting world: A star at
> dawn, a bubble in a stream; a flash of lightning in a sum-
> mer cloud, a flickering lamp, a phantom, and a dream.

When we are dying, we might say, "That was fast. What was that? I can't even grasp it. I don't know what it was." That is *nirvana*. Not trying to be enlightened is enlightenment. No thought of enlightenment is enlightenment. Enlightenment does not imply knowing. The moon is enlightenment. Knowing is delusion. We keep trying to turn the boat around and grab the shore.

When you decide to practice Zen meditation, it's actually very simple; you begin to see more deeply into who you really are. You begin to see the awakened part. The root of the word *buddha* is *budh*, which means "awake." Taking the precepts, the vows, is saying, "I want to practice living like the being I really am—the awake one."

Participating in this ritual of taking the precepts symbolizes a certain freedom. We do it in an old way. We can do it in a new way, too. Just sit down, come back to yourself, see what you really believe, and make a decision. "Okay, I'm doing this, so let's go. Let's take the boat out into the water and leave the shore behind." The Buddha calls it "crossing to the other shore." Then we find out that the other shore is this shore. This shore is the other shore.

In fifth- and sixth-century China, where Zen had its beginnings, the training was physically tough. We don't need to do it that way today, but we do need to be thorough and committed. That means learning to practice within our daily lives. We do this for ourselves. Tough training nurtures our determination. We sit hour after hour, sometimes in discomfort and fatigue, yet we have to persist. We have to be committed; we need the nourishment and energy that meditation brings. This doesn't have to be inflicted upon us by some authority figure. Look to yourself. We all need to look to ourselves to find the energy that will enable us to us cast off from the shore. The fact is, we've already cast off. We're going down the river from life to death. We have two choices: we can try to hold onto every rock, root, or island; or we can just let go and enjoy the ride, floating on the current. My version of the Lobster Quadrille goes like this:

> Will you, won't you, will you, won't you,
> Would have, could have, would have, should have joined
> the dance.

When I went into a Buddhist monastery for the first time, I threw myself completely into the experience. I had the wild and crazy energy of a rock 'n' roll star. It doesn't matter how you summon the energy, you just have to have it. Part of the history of our lineage is that the teachers have all had different temperaments, but they've all mustered the energy to persist in their practice.

Maezumi Roshi was an elegant intellectual. He was very strict about posture and form, but also really wanted people to enjoy the practice. He always reminded his students to "appreciate your life." Each teacher has a completely different energy and you can learn something from each one, it just might not be the thing you're expecting to learn.

Everybody's different; everybody has different karma, and everybody has something that you can learn from. One thing I learned from my teachers was that the key to the practice was not just sitting with the koans or even sitting and breathing mindfully, it was being willing to cast off, to leave whatever I thought of as home. It doesn't matter if you leave home as a determined warrior, a steadfast intellectual, or a wandering nomad; but you've got to leave home—the hometown of our concepts and beliefs.

The Buddha was the first person we know of who really got in the boat, cast off the lines, and left home. He was just a person. Just think of him as your best buddy; just think of him as you.

Four

GO HOME TO YOUR MOTHER

First it marked out a racecourse, in a sort of circle ("the exact shape doesn't matter," it said), and then all the party were placed along the course, here and there. There was no "One, two, three, and away," but they began running when they liked, and left off when they liked, so that it was not easy to know when the race was over. However, when they had been running half an hour or so, and were quite dry again, the Dodo suddenly called out "The race is over!" and they all crowded round it, panting, and asking, "But who has won?"

What is it to be a good Buddhist practitioner? Some of you think you know, and some of you think you don't know, and some of you may have never thought about it, or haven't done so for a long time. Deciding that you're going to be a practitioner of Zen is a very interesting decision to make with your life. It's wonderfully freeing. You simply decide you're going to practice until you die, and then you do it.

Once you've made the decision, nothing more can go wrong. Deciding to practice Buddhism settles the question of what you're going to do with your life. Nothing can disturb your determination to practice. Obstacles just become part of the practice. Your Zen practice will look different from someone else's. It may include "sitting" with and without koans, listening to Dharma talks, study, work practice in the kitchen, gardens, and office, daily mindfulness practice. It may also include arts practice and body practice, the study of the sutras, and the writings of the classical and contemporary Zen teachers as well as teachers from other traditions. But however you decide ultimately to practice, a large part of it will be working with what seem to be large obstacles.

When you reach these obstacles, you're simply going to practice with the faith that this is a good way to lead your life. It's a mistake to think this practice is going to make you different in some way or give you some kind of status. It's easy to forget that we aren't immortal. We're just travelers passing through.

"Leaving home" is a phrase that comes from the monastic tradition. It describes the commitment to go forth, to leave what's familiar and follow a spiritual path. It's a spirit you can follow as well. Leaving home doesn't mean leaving the world and it doesn't require living in a monastery. You're leaving behind the attitudes of the world. If you decide that your life is about practice, you're on your path. You're going to practice, no matter what else is going on.

Part of that inner decision is understanding that practice implies growth and change. Because of this, it's useful to have a teacher and a sangha, a community, so we don't remain frozen in time with some old understanding. To practice is to become empty so we can develop new understanding all the time. Practicing requires that you be open enough not to confine yourself to one idea about practice.

Practice has many aspects: meditation, the teacher-student relationship, talks, koan study. You do not have to belong to a monastery. Your practice can happen while you work and while you are at home, during your ordinary life. It helps if you learn and study basic mindfulness practices and develop close and harmonious relationships with other practitioners and with a teacher. This is important.

You shouldn't have to choose between your practice and your life. I learned this from experience. Instead, throw yourself fully into your life and into your practice. They will support one another and become the same thing. This also implies a certain amount of trust—trust that you can be guided, steered, given the right material, the right circumstances, and the right feedback to move your practice deeper. With trust, you can let someone else be your teacher and pilot the boat for a while. But it's still your boat.

Consistency over time is the hardest part. For example, whichever your beginning Buddhist practice emphasizes, sitting or koans or service, you'll tend to see that option as the right way to practice. But these things are not the practice, they are forms of the practice. An important aspect of practice is the ability to constantly relearn what the practice is—learning to not be stuck. We don't have a fixed idea. If we're practicing, we're not clinging to some idea of the self, to some form of the practice, or to some idea of what's good or bad about any of it.

When I was living in Zen Mountain Monastery, I had to pay housing and training fees. I lived in monastery housing with my wife, Caryn, and our five-year-old son, Alex. I was only allowed to work one day a week as a therapist; I saw ten people a day. Another day a week I was allowed to teach a workshop in meditative movement at a New Age center. I would teach this class after participating in intensive retreats that involved hours of sitting. I had no time to spend with my new family.

I had one day off a week, and if Daido Roshi was not around on that day I was often asked to give a talk. There was a donation request for the talk and lunch. When I passed the donation box I was told that I should make a donation—even though I was giving the talk. That was part of my training. And so it went for years. That is one way to practice. Now I can also see the benefits of throwing oneself into practice in daily life: appreciating your relationship, your work, every moment as a potential vehicle for awakening.

Genpo Roshi and his teacher, Maezumi Roshi, used to say, "Relinquish the self." I could say just the opposite, "Don't relinquish the self," but it wouldn't mean that I disagree with them. We all have a self. For some of us an obstacle to the practice is that we are filled with self-doubt, or that we don't spend enough time with ourselves. For others, it's that we are so full of ourselves there's no room for anything else. Unless we sit with the self, every little thing bats us around and we get lost. Maezumi Roshi and my teachers before him were not easygoing people. They were compassionate, but they weren't easygoing. We have to become strong and resilient, because if we aren't secure enough in ourselves and in our determination, we'll either quit the practice or be angry and resentful all the time.

Where I grew up, there were frequently fistfights in the streets, and sometimes I joined in. When you watch a fight, you can tell right away who has the most spirit (*chi* in Chinese, *ki* in Japanese). Chi is not arrogance, although sometimes it can manifest itself that way. It's not even confidence. I define it as undaunted spirit; a spirit you can't rattle. In the old martial arts tradition Bushidō, it's said you can have positive chi or negative chi.

We all have a current of this energy. When we interact with something, we interact with positive or negative chi. In our practice—this is a yang aspect of the teaching—it is the whispering of the lineage to push the student a little, sometimes in very subtle ways. If the teacher pushes too hard, the student falls on his back. If the teacher pushes just a little, the student pushes back and his spine gets stronger. The student is not pushing against the teacher, but against his own negative chi. He is undaunted.

> "Come back!" the Caterpillar called after her. "I've something important to say!"
>
> This sounded promising, certainly: Alice turned and came back again.
>
> "Keep your temper," said the Caterpillar.
>
> "Is that all?" said Alice, swallowing down her anger as well as she could.
>
> "No," said the Caterpillar.

When I studied martial arts I had a wonderful kung fu teacher named Willy Wo Luk—we called him Sifu, or master. The training was very hard: we used to say the class was divided into three parts—pain, agony, and suffering. We concluded the first part by doing push-ups on our fists and then on our fingertips. Often my pain and exhaustion were so great I couldn't finish the push-ups. One day, Sifu noticed this and began to teach me in earnest. Just as I was about to collapse, he got down on the floor and put his face right next to mine. Then he did one of the most wonderful things a human being has ever done for me. He said, "You can do it." He said it again and again. It brought tears to my eyes.

A couple of weeks later I was doing the required sparring for senior students (this follows the two hours of pain, agony, and suffering). When I finished I leaned against the wall and wiped the sweat from my brow. He walked over to me, cocked his head in what seemed like puzzlement and said, "Do you think this is a country club?" He was telling me that he expected more from me, that he believed in me. He was telling me that I had the ability to take my practice seriously.

Sifu had another tactic he employed when I would occasionally miss class without notifying him in advance; he would ignore me for several classes in a row. He was telling me that my commitment to him as a teacher was important in a way that went right to my heart. I still feel so much gratitude for his kindness.

People have all kinds of obstacles in their paths. Some people can't get up in the morning. When they ask me how to get up, I tell them to set the alarm clock and when the alarm rings, get out of bed. Don't consider the mysteries of the universe, don't question why you're doing this, don't contemplate how you feel—simply get up and go. Some people are very good at doing that, others aren't. Some of us are closed. Some of us are good at being open. Some of us are getting better. That's our practice. That's where our chi needs to go, against the negative part of us that won't open so we can actually relinquish that part of the self.

"What matters it how far we go?" his scaly friend replied,
"There is another shore, you know, upon the other side."

Some of us are afraid. We don't want to step forward and declare ourselves. We don't feel good enough about ourselves to do that, and that is a sad thing. There is not a single person in the world who cannot be a fine practitioner.

In the Soto Zen tradition I come from, when a person feels like they are ready to become more commited to their Buddhist practice, they take *jukai*. Jukai is a formal rite of passage that marks entrance into the Buddhist community. At that time, a student is given a dharma name, and makes a commitment to the Three Pure Precepts and the Ten Grave Precepts.

The Three Pure Precepts

1. Not Creating Evil
2. Practicing Good
3. Actualizing Good for Others

The Ten Grave Precepts

1. Affirm life. Do not kill
2. Be giving. Do not steal
3. Honor the body. Do not misuse sexuality
4. Manifest truth. Do not lie
5. Proceed clearly. Do not cloud the mind
6. See the perfection. Do not speak of others' errors and faults
7. Realize self and other as one. Do not elevate the self and blame others
8. Give generously. Do not be withholding
9. Actualize harmony. Do not be angry
10. Experience the intimacy of things. Do not defile the Three Treasures (Buddha, Dharma, and Sangha)

When we have practiced for a while, we usually look back and see that the beginning of our understanding started when we received jukai. Making this solid and serious commitment plants a seed of understanding that only continues to grow as we continue to practice.

In Zen practice, we talk about the lineage of practitioners. We look back at generation after generation who've spent their lives practicing. There are many that are documented and there were many others we know very little about. For example, in Japan there was a women's lineage. It is important to understand that in any human endeavor there are countless numbers of nameless unknowns—women, men, and children of all races, religions, cultures, and economic backgrounds, even animals and plants—that we owe so much gratitude to. The best way to repay them is to appreciate them and honor their lives with our own conscious effort to wake up.

Thomas Cleary's book *Timeless Spring: A Soto Zen Anthology* is about the lineage of the Soto school of Zen. I thought it was depressing when I first read it at the age of thirty. I didn't like reading about death. Dying was not yet on my horizon. Today I enjoy thinking about the way these people lived and practiced and died. They practiced for thirty years, they realized the teaching, and they spent their lives passing it on. Then the teaching was passed on again. That sounds wonderful. It's wonderful to embrace that process and commit to supporting it. And while we do that we can also learn to appreciate everything in our lives.

Genpo Roshi once held a sesshin that I attended. Afterward, we all went to a Chinese restaurant for dinner. The woman who was the *tenzo*, or cook, during the sesshin was a dedicated Zen practitioner, a wonderful person, and a marvelous tenzo. She leaned over and asked me, "Are you into the Mother?" (She was talking about Guru Mai, a very popular guru.) I turned to her and said, "No." She said, "I am." I said, "That's good." I didn't want to ask anything else, as I was afraid it would turn the conversation sour. I was a new practitioner and she was a real role model to me. She had been raised in a horsey, upper-class Connecticut milieu, but had somehow become spiritualized at an early age and was devoted to her practice. Every day I used to watch her go into the kitchen, prepare food, put the food out, and take a nap. And every single day she'd go back and do it again. She seemed completely content. My girlfriend used to tease me that I had a crush on the tenzo, and I did. I regarded her as a relentless practitioner. I admired her for that.

Later, I read Master Dogen's book on the tenzo and refining your life. There's a famous story in which an old tenzo is pounding the rice and Dogen says to him, "Why are you pounding this rice at your age?" And the tenzo says, "If I don't do it, who will?" In one way, this is a satisfying answer and in another way, it's not. It's satisfying because it's important to carry on the practice for the benefit of others. We emphasize that side of practice a lot. But I also like to emphasize the other side—the side that says to practice for yourself; practice because you choose to lead the life of a practitioner, because it is one of the most wonderful, pleasurable existences you can choose. Do it for selfish reasons and it will benefit everyone.

There's no reason you have to choose between practicing Zen and enjoyment. We don't have to approach being a practitioner of Zen as an ascetic. I'm not talking about fun. I'm talking about *real* pleasure, elegant pleasure as opposed to the coarse, unfulfilling stuff that gives you a hangover. Do we have the prejudice that this practice is not pleasure? It *is* pleasure. We get pleasure from sitting. Then we walk outside and we look at the snow and the blue sky and we see it in a different way. To have that subtle, fine, clear sight that the dharma gives is pleasure—quiet and empty.

It's not possible to feel any better than your body and mind feel. If the body is as healthy and relaxed as it can be and the mind is easy and relaxed and open, what can be better than that? A lot of people would like to convince you that there are better things, because your interest in those things makes money for them. But the real beauty in our lives, the most exquisite realization, is in the smallest, quietest, simplest things. Your mind quiet. A leaf falling.

When the Mock Turtle sings of his soup, he could be Walt Whitman singing his "Song of Myself":

> Beautiful soup so rich and green,
> Waiting in a hot tureen!
> Who for such dainties would not stoop?
> Soup of the evening, beautiful soup!
> Soup of the evening, beautiful soup!

Many of our spiritual ancestors have tried to communicate the pleasure of the moment. In the collection of koans called the Blue Cliff Record,

Master Chosha says, "First I went following the fragrant grasses and now I have returned in pursuit of the falling blossoms." To which the head monk responds, "You are full of the spring."

When Zen masters speak of "not going anywhere" it means the mind isn't going anywhere, isn't seeking after anything, and so the mind isn't agitated. We sometimes practice to get to that quiet mind because we think it's a good thing to do, something that will develop us, or something the teacher wants. But perhaps we don't realize often enough that it's where the real joy in life is. We think a quiet, aware mind isn't sexy or compelling enough. It's just such a quiet thing, and we're told we don't want that well of quiet. We hear about answers. What was the question? We look for meaning. What is meaning? What is the meaning of love? What is the meaning of rain?

I heard a story about a pianist who was giving a performance of twentieth-century classical music. The harmonies in the composition were dissonant and some people found it difficult to listen to. After she was through playing the piece, an audience member raised his hand and asked, "What does that mean?" The pianist just played the piece again.

When we stop searching and sit in the silence of the moment, you may find a vast reservoir of incredible determination and spirit. For the ancient samurai, honor was more important than life and death; beauty was more important than life and death. What I'm suggesting is that practice can be more important than life and death. As Master Dogen would say, "To become one with practice is to become one with enlightenment." Practice and enlightenment are the same thing.

In the movie *Kill Bill 2*, we discover that the heroine, Ms. Kiddo, has just defeated a large number of *yakuza*, or Japanese gangsters. This dramatization of a seemingly violent event is actually intended to be humorous. In the end there is one very young gangster left holding a sword. She whacks the sword away, turns him over, spanks him, gives him his sword back, and says, "That's what you get for hanging out with bad people. Go home to your mother."

It was so simple. The little gangster had simply lost his way. When we become agitated and bent out of shape because we want ridiculous things, we should go home to our mother. I'm not referring to the practical things everybody needs in life. It's good to have enough food and shelter and warmth. But to endlessly chase after money believing that our happiness will come only when we have more and more is silly; and besides, it doesn't work. Our mind is the mother. Go home to Mother.

We've been given a wonderful gift and it's not even a gift; it just is. We have the power to practice with a little positive chi. Very slowly, through many years, through many winters and many storms, we gradually become the masters of our own minds. When our mind starts to get quiet, its buttons can't be pushed so easily. Some of the fear of life and death starts to drop away.

There are so many great things in life and we should appreciate them all; just don't forget who your mother is. You should know from sitting that deep commitment—the deep understanding and maturity to understand where the source is—makes the practice different. Don't despise success in people. Don't be for it, but don't be against it. That's what the ancestors tell us. Don't be for or against anything.

We choose enlightenment. We choose delusion. We don't choose enlightenment. We don't choose delusion. Deep understanding is no under-standing.

> "If there's no meaning in it," said the King, "that saves us a world of trouble, you know, as we needn't try to find any."

When we get married, the bond we feel with our partner doesn't begin at the time of the marriage. It already exists; we're already connected to our partner. The marriage ceremony doesn't create our feelings; it simply makes them visible. In the same way, if our practice is the answer to our life, we reveal our connection to the body of humankind. We're not creating a connection; one already exists. We have a deep relationship with the whole body of humanity. Committing ourselves to the practice—and again, this is practice year after year after year—enables us to open ourselves to the body of humanity, open to a oneness that is becoming increasingly clear. When our interactions with other human beings are based in our practice, they become something spiritual. This kind of energy is a certain field of the mind, something that's already there in us. Nobody's going to be fully awakened in a day or a year or ten years or twenty years, but we're home now. We've found our mother. We've found the source of beauty and real relationships to people.

Then we practice leaving home. But what's leaving home? It's coming home to ourselves. Nobody should be afraid to come home. Home is not about other people. It's about finding the most pleasurable, peaceful, beautiful, honorable, and altruistic way you can live your life and then committing to it. You have nothing to worry about. If you want to be a Buddha, that's okay too. Mind is buddha. Mind is Mother. Now go home to your mother.

Five

BEER PONG

"Well, I should like to be a little larger, sir, if you wouldn't mind,"
said Alice; "three inches is such a wretched height to be."

"It is a very good height indeed!" said the Caterpillar angrily,
rearing itself upright as it spoke (it was exactly three inches high).

My Zen lineage descends from both the Rinzai and the Soto lines of Zen. I've embraced the softer style of teaching usually associated with the Soto school, and the ways of spiritual self-development that are common in the Rinzai school. None of this is set in stone, of course, but Rinzai teachers often take great interest in the arts, tea ceremony, and music, and also in the warrior trainings: sword, karate, judo. Traditional Japanese martial arts training is often thought of as a journey from soft or receptive mind to no mind. There are many teaching stories associated with this journey.

There's a story from medieval Japan in which a young man goes out to study with a sword master. The teacher has him bring meals and carry other things, but doesn't teach him anything about the sword.

Eventually the student complains. The sword teacher says nothing. One day the student lies down to take a nap, and while he's sleeping, the teacher takes a broom and whacks him. Now this is feudal Japan, so this young man has to do whatever he signed up for, whether he likes it or not. The next day when he's cooking soup, the teacher comes up from behind and hits him with a spoon. From then on, whether the student is asleep or awake, the teacher attacks him with an object every chance he gets. This drives the student nuts. He says to the teacher, "This isn't what I signed up for." (If you practice Buddhism, you'll often hear some form of the phrase: "This isn't what I signed up for.")

So, the teacher keeps hitting the student, and this goes on for a long time, probably because the student is a good student and just can't quit. One day the student is making soup in a pot over a fire and the teacher comes up behind him with a big stick. Just as the teacher starts to strike, the student whips the lid off the pot and blocks it. This happens two or three times. The teacher tries to get the student in his sleep, but the student rolls over before he gets hit. Soon the teacher isn't able to hit him at all. And at that point the teacher says, "Now it's time to begin your formal sword training."

The sword was seen as an extension of the spirit in medieval Japan. Training has not changed very much. I once studied jazz piano with John Esposito, a wonderful teacher. My one-hour lessons always turned into three-hour lessons because he was so devoted to the music and because his spirit was so strong. Once I was struggling with a piece he wanted me to learn. I kept getting frustrated and finally asked him, "Is this part in the left hand or the right hand?" He smiled. Without saying a word he sat next to me on the piano bench and let me struggle with it some more. After a while he asked me if I knew which hand the piece was in. I said I still didn't. He pointed to my heart, and said, "It's in that hand."

Like Alice, I have often found that things are not what they seem to be. Sometimes we are the ones who create our own difficulties.

> A large rose tree stood near the entrance of the garden; the
> roses growing on it were white, but there were three gardeners
> at it, busily painting them red.

Genpo Roshi is always teaching. One time I was at his house, and he launched into a twenty-minute discussion about the yield sign on the corner of his block and how cars kept going through it even though the sign was clearly posted. Three months later, I realized he'd been talking about me.

The irony of this kind of teaching is that it's so much fun to sit around and laugh about it and so little fun to actually receive it. When you study, you spend a lot of time around your teacher. And nothing is less pleasant because it's not easy to learn things your ego doesn't want to learn. Nobody wants to hear that they should be doing things differently, or that what they just said was inappropriate, or that their understanding is not deep enough, or that they're not embodying the teaching.

It's very hard to teach people who have studied for a long time, because they don't think they have anything to learn. So we call the good students stupid. They're the ones who don't know anything. It's good to be stupid. If you don't get it in this context, think about it in your relationships. Would you rather have a relationship with someone who's infinitely smart and doesn't want to hear anything you have to say, or with someone who listens to you?

The historical Buddha was born in northern India. His name was Siddhartha Gautama and he was from a prominent royal family of the Shakya clan. He married at nineteen and had a pretty easy time of it until, one day when he was about twenty-eight, he was out with his charioteer. He saw sick people, people with missing limbs, suffering people, dying people; the charioteer said, "This is life. This is what happens. And it will happen to you, too." At that point, Siddhartha realized that he had been living his life as if in a dream, and he left his home and his family to see if he could learn to wake himself up.

This also is true for us: we're all going to die. But we don't think about that. We think about other things. A lot of the major religious and spiritual figures had sudden conversion experiences when they became ill. I did too. I'd been a Zen student for eighteen years when I became paralyzed from Guillain-Barré syndrome. For two years, I could barely move, even to speak. On Christmas Eve when I thought I'd recovered, I got up to walk and broke my foot. My paralysis became more profound over the next few months. At one point, I was as immobile as a log.

When I broke my foot, I had to go to the hospital. It's no fun being in the hospital on Christmas because nobody wants to work that day. The hospitals send in their grumpiest workers. It was terrible. Later, they were putting blood in my system and taking it out, which is a procedure called plasmapheresis. Your blood pressure has to stay even or you can die. Mine didn't stay even. I asked one of the nurses how low my blood pressure had gotten. "About twenty over ten," she said.

At that point I reached a new understanding of what was happening to me. I was going to die. If not now, then later. I am going to get sick and I am going to die. I think that's what Siddhartha understood; it wasn't just anybody who was going to get sick and die; *he* was going to get sick and *he* was going to die. That's when he decided to look for answers.

When he set out, he noticed a lot of other people wandering around who'd left home to pursue some form of spiritual practice. A lot of them practiced asceticism—they didn't eat meat or dairy and ate very few vegetables, and they sat until they hurt. They twisted their bodies into strange postures and sometimes they even whipped themselves. Siddhartha practiced asceticism for a long time.

A couple of years ago Caryn and I and our son Alex went to our niece's wedding in Rhode Island. What I really like to do in Rhode Island is complain about the West. I complained about the weather here in Utah: the sun, the seasons, the snow, and stuff like that. Then, when I'm home in Utah, I like to complain about Rhode Island.

You might think there's a kind of stupid cleverness going on here. By complaining about the other place, you're happier where you are. It's as if as soon as I go to Rhode Island, I decide to complain about the West so I can try to be happy in Rhode Island. It isn't easy.

"Not the same thing a bit!" said the Hatter. "You might just as well
say that 'I see what I eat' is the same thing as 'I eat what I see'!"
"You might just as well say," added the March Hare, "that 'I like
what I get' is the same thing as 'I get what I like'!"

At the wedding, some of the younger people stayed up and played
a game called beer pong. In beer pong you line up some glasses full
of beer on either side of a table. One team stands on each side of the
table, and one at a time the members throw a Ping-Pong ball, trying
to get it inside the beer glasses on the opposite side of the table. If your
team succeeds, the other team drinks the glasses of beer. If your team
misses, you drink the beer. After a little while, everyone just drinks at
will.

There was probably an ancient form of beer pong that Siddhartha
gave up in order to search for truth. Siddhartha had seen that his life
was going to involve disease, old age, and death. He saw that he and
everybody around him were just playing beer pong, and at a certain
point, he said, "Okay, this is not it. I would like to know more. I can't
just sit around doing this and waiting to get old and die." Maybe he
was just more sensitive or scared than other people. He wanted to solve
the question of death.

After practicing asceticism for some time, Siddhartha took a more
moderate approach toward his physical needs. He made it his practice to
see through reality. And he came to see that everything is one. Not only
that he was one with everything, but so was everyone else. He decided
he would try to share this knowledge with others.

At first, he thought it would be impossible. What he had learned was unexplainable in words and could only be experienced. When he went out and told people about it, some were open to listening to him and to the notion that they, too, had the capacity to wake up.

After a lot of drinking and beer pong, the wedding took place and my niece, Jessie, married her boyfriend. They'd been living together for seven years and they were ready. This is life for many of us in the West: we have children, we have families, we play beer pong, we get old, we get sick, and then we die.

The reason the Buddha didn't know the meaning of life was the same reason we don't—he thought he already knew the meaning of life. He was surrounded by a society that told him what everything was.

When the Buddha finally sat down and went through his process of meditation, he didn't learn anything. He unlearned everything. He dropped all his thoughts, his associations, and his favorite things. And one morning, after he had meditated so long and hard, for a moment he knew nothing. And in that moment of knowing nothing, he looked at the morning star and there was no separation between him and the star. There was no separation between him and anything else. There was no time, no space, no nothing. There was one thing, and everything he knew of himself from before seemed like a dream. It's as if he said, "I fell asleep and dreamed I was Siddhartha Gautama of the Shakya clan, and forgot that I was the absolute." He recognized that everyone around him was having this same dream, that they all thought they were a creature with a separate identity, someone who suffers and dies, just passes through the universe and then is gone.

The Buddha thought he should tell others about his insight, but he didn't know how. He assumed people wouldn't believe him if he were to tell them that they were the absolute! That they were everything! He didn't know how to communicate something beyond words, so he spent about four days not telling people. Then he decided to try. He spent the rest of his life practicing and teaching.

There was no such thing as Buddhism in the days of the Buddha. The Buddha was simply a person who realized who he was. In the moment when the Buddha realized himself, he was neither old, young, male, female, Indian, black, white, or brown. The person who realized himself, who awakened at that time, was you. Most of the time, you don't walk around saying you're thirty-seven or fifty-seven or you're a man or you're a woman—you're just you, right? At the time of realization, the Buddha was you in your deepest part, not the part that is your thoughts.

At the wedding in Rhode Island, after everybody drank for a while, we danced. We laughed. We slapped each other on the back, hugged, and danced some more.

The Buddha saw that things are transient. He saw that everything— our good times, our jobs, the people we marry—is allocated a certain period of time, and then it goes away.

After the wedding we flew home through Chicago, but due to a storm our plane was grounded. We couldn't leave. I was very happy being on that plane because I got to spend three hours reading. I don't get a lot of undisturbed time. Finally, they told us to get off because the plane wasn't going anywhere. Now there were two thousand people from various flights trying to get hotel rooms. Two thousand people were ready to kill each other to get on the bus; they were ready to walk— shoving and screaming—over bodies. Such situations are also a part of life. While we wait for life to change into something more idyllic, something more to our liking, it goes by.

Eventually, we got a ride to a hotel. The guy who drove us to the hotel was a friendly fellow, but he liked to smoke with the windows closed. I haven't smoked for years, so it was really pleasant to be able to inhale. When we got to the hotel, there was a line of people and a three-hour wait to get a room. The hotel was hosting a darts tournament. There were hundreds of people from the Midwest, all drunk and throwing darts.

> "I don't think they play at all fairly," Alice began, in rather a
> complaining tone, "and they all quarrel so dreadfully one can't
> hear oneself speak—and they don't seem to have any rules in
> particular; at least, if there are, nobody attends to them."

In that unfamiliar Chicago hotel room, I felt utterly unmoored and also, oddly, at home. I thought of Siddhartha wandering through the countryside of India. The strange and familiar complexity of the human condition is always showing itself, wherever we are. We find our stability in our breath, in our awareness of the current moment as the only moment.

When the Buddha realized who he was, he saw his oneness with everything and he felt at home anywhere. His practice was to continually remind himself: *this* is nirvana, *this* is enlightenment, this—*my life*—is enlightenment. If he'd gone to Timbuktu, he would have liked it there, if he'd gone to Korea he would've liked it there, and if he were based in Utah, he'd have liked it there too. Wherever the Buddha went, he was at home. He'd found that the way to liberation, the way out of life and death and disease, is to be exactly where you are, going nowhere. Because when a person is exactly where they are, going nowhere, they're at peace, they're happy, and they're one—even in Rhode Island.

In the Soto Zen tradition, we call the practice of sitting *shikantaza*. *Shikan* means "only" or "one with" and *taza* means "sitting." Just sitting. Sitting for itself, not for something else. We don't sit to attain enlightenment, because we all already have the capacity for enlightenment. We sit to sit, and in doing so we experience our own already-present awareness of the connectedness of all things. When we use the word shikan by itself, it means that wherever you are, whatever you're doing, at any moment of your life you are simply "one with."

When we can become one with whatever we're doing, there's nothing outside it, there's nothing to compare it to, there's nothing to worry about, there's nothing else. At this very moment, if you simply stop looking, relax, and accept, you are shikan. If you don't look for anything or try to figure anything out, if you just take a deep breath and simply *are*, right here, this is the Buddha. You are the Buddha. There's nothing further to know. This is nirvana; this is the other shore. Every bit of it, every moment is the other shore. The reason we don't reach the other shore is that we keep trying to get to the other shore. This *is* the other shore.

Six

DON'T PLAY THE BUTTER NOTES

"I only took the regular course."

"What was that?" inquired Alice.

"Reeling and Writhing, of course, to begin with," the Mock
Turtle replied; "and then the different branches of Arithmetic—
Ambition, Distraction, Uglification, and Derision."

When I began to practice at Zen Mountain Monastery, I had an experience that surprised me. I was sitting a long retreat and after almost a week of sitting I realized that everything I thought, everything I had been taught, was just a belief. I was looking to find something out; and instead I had a wonderful moment when all my ideas left. I felt so free. I didn't need to believe anything. I got out from under all my so-called knowledge. I saw that I'd been binding myself without a rope. I've never forgotten that.

What sometimes happens when you teach, is that people go right into their feelings and they have an emotional reaction. When that happens, they don't get the message; they misinterpret it to mean that you "approve" or "disapprove" of them. As a student, I've had that experience with my teacher Genpo Roshi countless times. It's too bad, because approval and disapproval are insignificant. What's important is to get the message. It's not my desire to upset anybody. Dogen said we study with no mind and we study with the mind. And I'm saying, don't dumb down the practice. We can use the mind if we're not busy being used by it.

In a radio interview, Herbie Hancock once described an exchange he had with Miles Davis. Miles was a great teacher. Herbie had just started playing with the Miles Davis Quintet, but he wasn't quite getting the sound Miles wanted. One day Miles, who was known for giving cryptic instructions to his band members, leaned over to Herbie and said, in his hoarse voice, "Don't play the butter notes." Herbie had to think about this for a while before he finally got it. The message, he realized, was don't play what comes most easily, most mechanically. He said it changed his playing for good.

Recently I went on retreat to a beautiful place called Hatch Point in the desert of southern Utah. Retreats offer a teacher an opportunity to observe his or her own practice as well as to observe others practicing and see how they react in different situations. All of us have areas in which we get stuck, and by observing ourselves, we can slip out of our stuck spots, or as Master Rinzai puts it, "untie knots." Sometimes it takes going away, taking a break from our regular lives, to help us untie the tightest of knots.

At the retreat, we did an empowerment ceremony. We formed a circle and everyone bowed to each person, one by one. Through a series of chants, bows, and walking meditation, the community honored the true nature of each being. We did this in part to acknowledge that without our community, our sangha, there can be no awakening. There is no such thing as individual enlightenment.

Sometimes we can practice in parallel but not develop any intimacy with each other. But if we do not also practice how to relate to and communicate with others, then we are not really practicing Buddhism. The sangha holds the key. The sangha is a wonderful tool, because, over time, it reveals you to yourself. Whatever you are, whatever your "stuff" is, wherever you're stuck, if you stay long enough, everybody in the sangha will know about it—including you.

The sangha is an exceptionally multifaceted teaching device. Be open to it. The sangha can teach us to see ourselves, to have perspective. If one person says you're a horse, you might be a horse; if two people say you're a horse, you might be a horse; but if three people say you're a horse, you'd better get a saddle. The less of yourself you expose, the slower it goes. If you're conscious, you begin to see the ego as well as that which transcends the ego. In this way you use the mind to study the self.

The mind manifests itself in many ways. The mind of faith in practice is the mind of *shuke*, the mind that leaves home. Home is whatever you think it is, and we leave it in different ways. Along with several others, I left my physical home to come to Utah so we could practice at Kanzeon Zen Center. We left our jobs, our friends, our sources of income. "Leaving mind" means that, in order to practice, you leave behind your old mind and the things that are attached to it. If you give up nothing for this practice, you don't create a vessel in which to put something.

Each of us has to give up different things. Some of us have to give up our anger; some of us have to give up our hometown; some of us have to give up being worried or scared; some of us have to give up our insensitivity to others. After practicing for a long time, we start to see what a cesspool our mind can be. We start to see how the mind, left to its own devices without practice or study of the self, is not a very happy place. It takes a long time to see that. If we look at it closely, we find fear. Fear puts a wall between ourselves and our life. Fear hurts us and paralyzes us. We are so often in a state of fear—or its cousin, anxiety—that we don't even know it. We just act out of that place. We act out our insecurities, our projections, our anger. We're not conscious of it. We play the butter notes.

One of my students told me she realized she had a strong desire to be recognized as a special person, a high achiever. That was very good because she was conscious of her desire and she voiced it. Most of us just act on our desires. If a person comes in and starts to practice and wants to be recognized as special, unique, better, I have news for him—that is average, ordinary, the usual. A person who comes in with no desire to be special, superior, or recognized: now *that's* unusual, extraordinary, and special. Do you know anyone like that?

When we study Zen with the body, we do it in at least two ways. One way is to find the true human body—the body that includes the stars, the wind, the desert. The true human body has no limits, no edges, no size, no shape; it includes everything. We are born, conditioned, and then we forget the true human body, the body of the Buddha. If you can forget the self, the true human body emerges fully blooming, like a flower. At the same time, to realize the true human body, we have to use this lump of flesh, this physical body, because these two kinds of bodies are one and the same. Is this a problem? I don't think so.

Practice at Zen Mountain Monastery was physically grueling. That kind of rigorous practice can encourage some of our old habits. Some of us in the sangha disregarded compassion for ourselves. We would just sit and sit and sit and push our bodies and grow tired. People who train in that way can endure, but simple endurance is not Zen practice. Full awareness of the moment as it exists is Zen practice.

There's a line in "The Hedgehog Song" by the Incredible String Band: "You know all the words and sing all the notes, but you never quite learned the song." In our practice, we can play all the notes and we can say all the words, but it's not the song. The ways we practice are the notes, but how do we really make the song? One way is to be sincere.

When you practice, as Dogen Zenji says, practice with the body and with the mind. Don't practice with some little piece of yourself. It's not enough to practice realization just by opening our eyes. We have to practice being the Awakened Mind. The sangha is the perfect teaching device and the mirror that allows us to see the reality of our practice.

I finished my formal training after twenty-five years of practice. Genpo Roshi then began to tell me how important the support of the sangha is for a teacher. He was preparing me to be a teacher: a process referred to as "transmission." I was running the Zen Center and beginning to teach, and I was really stuck in the butter notes. I had gotten so involved in my own performance and in the abstract concept, "for the good of the center," that I was not really seeing or connecting to the community and the people around me. Genpo Roshi has said to me that if you put someone in the sangha in a position of leadership but the sangha doesn't trust the leader, they will pull the person down by their feet. If the sangha feels the leadership is genuine, they will push the person up.

Something important happened after this. I started to look at the people around me, and I began to like and care for them and treat them kindly. The next thing I knew, my life changed. On the day Genpo Roshi announced in the zendo that he was going to transmit to me, the sangha applauded, which was something very rare. It was a wonderful moment in my own understanding of the importance of sangha. Then Daido Roshi, my old teacher, came out to Utah to do the transmission ceremony with Genpo. I hope to pass on this experience, and the attitudes and understanding I got from it, to my own students. The sangha, if we let it, will awaken to embody the Buddha.

The Chinese character for the word "enlightenment" is made from the combined characters for "sun" and "moon." Enlightenment is the yoking of the two together. This is practicing with the mind of true appreciation: the mind that appreciates life and death as enlightenment; this shore as the other shore; this flesh as the true human body; this day as a good day. What stops us from realizing this mind of appreciation is the gap between our concepts and enlightenment. To practice is to close this gap. Wishing to close this gap is the mind of practice. The sangha can help us. It can reflect the gaps for us. The wisdom in other people's view of us can make us more objective about our behaviors and more sensitive to others. If we're open, it can help us embody and manifest the practice—close the gap.

Dogen Zenji says we should practice with the body. When we get up tomorrow, instead of having our usual fearful, angry, irritated thoughts, we may, as Tinkerbell says when Peter Pan is sick, "think good thoughts." Thinking good thoughts is really just un-sticking ourselves from our habitual thinking patterns. Suddenly, because you're thinking good thoughts, you'll find that it is a good day. You won't be so bothered by the fact that everybody else may be thinking bad thoughts. But "good" and "bad" are misleading terms. What we're really talking about is the absence of fear and anger and the presence of empathy and intimacy. We can think good thoughts about bad thoughts. One word for that is compassion. We can act on it with our bodies and with our words, but we need to practice kicking our greed, anger, and ignorance—our "bad" or "stuck" thoughts, our fear. Only someone who is going to live forever has time for fear. For those of us just passing through, being caught in our fear is a terrible waste of time. Fear is natural. Being caught in fear is nonproductive.

It's difficult to have compassion for others if you're not feeling good or if your mind is full of anger and irritation. So your practice has to start in the body. What we can do in our human bodies is be real in our practice. Be truthful. Be conscious of what our state is and how the state of our body and mind affects others. I don't think we'll ever reach a point where we have nothing more to learn; so this means ongoing practice and learning, being open, and having some humility.

An old Sufi tale tells of the fabled Mullah Nasreddin—who is known by different names in different cultures. The wise mullah becomes a judge. A woman comes before him with her child and says, "This kid eats sugar all the time. I can't trust him. He goes into the sugar bowl, he's addicted to sugar." Mullah Nasreddin listens and says, "Court is adjourned. Come back in two weeks." When the court reconvenes the mullah issues his verdict, saying, "The child must restrict himself to two spoons of sugar a day." The mother asks why the case was adjourned for two weeks, and the mullah says, "Before I decided on a verdict I had to get down to two spoons myself."

The night sky out in the desert at Hatch Point is full of stars. The stars stretch from the very bottom of the horizon all the way up to the top of the sky. Someone at the retreat I attended said it was reassuring to her that this sky is the same sky she saw when she was a child. The Milky Way and all the constellations are still there.

That's true. It's also true that there's a lot of action out there we don't see from here. We've developed this idea of what our mind is, what our body is, what we can reach, and what we can affect. We begin to think we understand the world around us, but there's so much we just don't know.

> "I can't explain MYSELF, I'm afraid, sir," said Alice, "because I'm
> not myself you see."
> "I don't see," said the Caterpillar.
> "I'm afraid I can't put it more clearly," Alice replied very politely,
> "for I can't understand it myself to begin with."

Maezumi Roshi felt that in our time the sangha would be the most important of the Three Treasures, which are the Buddha, the dharma, and the sangha. The Buddha is the Awakened One; the dharma is the teaching; and the sangha is the practicing community. Our connection with the sangha supports us in the difficulties of the practice.

In the fairy tale "The Emperor's New Clothes," the emperor walks around asking, "How do you like my new clothes?" and everyone says, "They're great!" But then a little boy asks, "Mommy, why is the emperor naked?" The sangha is there to make sure we don't walk around admiring new clothes that we're not even wearing.

When people who have been practicing for many years appear angry, insensitive, or superior, new practitioners may wonder, "If that's what you guys produce after so many years of practicing, why should we do this practice?" Without a sangha that reflects us back to ourselves, we could continue practicing for a long time, thinking we're becoming an enlightened, compassionate being while we appear to others as angry and insensitive.

Sometimes we're still stuck, even after many years of practice. Instead of really leaving our homes, we just redecorate the walls. But the sangha can help us get perspective. Experience with the sangha, and with others in our lives, can help us see the causes and consequences of our actions and words, and even of our thoughts that come across as attitudes. It can be shocking how quickly our unconscious actions come back to us.

"No, no!" said the Queen. "Sentence first—verdict afterward."

I used to be a fierce zendo monitor at Zen Mountain Monastery. I didn't gain much from yelling at people in the zendo and I don't think they appreciated it, but they learned to endure. Now I'm asking you to be fierce with your practice. If you want to succeed, you're going to have to endure; not just talk the talk, but walk the walk, do the practice. This requires not doing what comes automatically. It requires taking responsibility for our own development and not blaming others for our state. It's wonderful to forget all of the negative rules that limit our experience. That's what happened to Alice. No matter how talented we are, it's going to take time, but we can help each other.

Just don't play the butter notes.

Seven

THE WORLD'S LARGEST KALEIDOSCOPE

Alice laughed. "There's no use trying," she said. "One can't believe impossible things."

"I dare say you haven't had much practice," said the Queen. "When I was your age I always did it for half an hour a day. Why sometimes I've believed as many as six impossible things before breakfast."

When I was nine years old, I went with my mother to the post office to buy stamps. The post office displayed posters of people wanted by the FBI, and as we waited in line I read their descriptions. These people looked scary. The things they'd done were scary. That night when I went to bed, it occurred to me that any one of these criminals could climb onto the fire escape outside my window and come into my room. I was terrified. But in the middle of being terrified, I had this thought: Why am I me? How did I get to be the center of the universe? I'm just an individual person on the planet, but I got into the role of being me; which, for me, is the center of the universe.

In the collection of Buddhist scriptures called the Majjhima Nikaya, the Buddha describes a defining moment:

> When I was a young man, at the beginning of my life,
> I looked at nature and saw that all things are subject to
> decay and death and thus to sorrow. The thought came to
> me that I myself was of such a nature. I was the same as
> all created things. I too would be subject to disease, decay,
> death, and sorrow. But what if I were to search for that
> which underlies all becoming, for the unsurpassed per-
> fect security which is nirvana, the perfect freedom of the
> unconditioned state? So, in the first flush of my indepen-
> dence, I went against my father's wishes.

I could never explain my epiphany to anyone. Nevertheless, it was an event. In a way, it was touching enlightenment for a moment. I was questioning and seeing my identity clearly for the first time. This first insight was correct—namely, that each of us feels we are the center of the universe. Aside from encompassing the universe, we are each the center of it.

Why is that? Why are things arranged in such a way that each of us feels we are the center of the universe? Why doesn't anyone else acknowledge that we're the center of the universe? Why does everybody think *they're* the center of the universe? What's going on? What is it to awaken?

We think of the historical Buddha as Siddhartha, and perhaps that exotic name puts him at a distance from us. But we don't need distance, we need intimacy; we need the dharma to be here today. So let's call him Sid. Sid was just a regular guy, but he was also a rebel. He was a counterculture type—perhaps in a different time he would have been seen as a beatnik like Jack Kerouac, Gary Snyder, Allen Ginsberg, Anne Waldman, or Michael McClure.

The Buddha's father was a regional king, and Indian society was very strict. Even today Indian life is pretty strict. Some Indians are just now having their first non-arranged marriages—even those whose families have been in the U.S. for a couple of generations. Sid went against his parents' wishes when he left home. When he went out into the world, he saw people who were sick and dying, and he thought, "I don't want this to happen." I don't blame him for having these feelings. I don't want it to happen either.

He also saw people hanging out in the streets meditating or doing yoga. That was the counterculture of the time. Sid fell in with them and went to live in a park—Deer Park. They were living a countercultural life with people who thought there was a way to transcend the normal everyday kinds of things that make us all suffer.

Sid, the Buddha, was also a very high achiever. He took on the impossible. He decided he was going to solve the biggest problem in the world—the problem of life and death. The Buddha did something remarkable—and this is our legacy—he lifted up the veil that covered his own mind. This is an awareness anyone can train to have. It doesn't require anything but mind and the desire to overcome conditioning or suffering.

The Buddha didn't identify with being a buddha, nor did he identify with being a Buddhist. There was no Buddhism yet. He also didn't identify with being what Carlos Castaneda's Yaqui sage, Don Juan, calls an "immortal being." Don Juan tells his student Carlos that immortal beings are the regular people who live their lives as if they're not going to die. This means we live our lives as if doing what everybody says we ought to do is going to lead to a good outcome, like retirement, or a better job, or winning the lottery. Our achievements are good, they satisfy us, but only in part. Even a belief that someday we'll be so satisfied we'll walk around with a permanent grin on our face puts us at odds with life. It isn't going to happen. The Buddha didn't believe any of that. If we're still attached to thinking that our achievements are more important than realizing our true nature, we ought to look at that. If we believe that we're going to find a way to separate everything good in life from everything we think is bad, we need to look at that. What Sid realized was that he was the only thing between heaven and Earth. It was all him—and he is us.

As the Buddha says in the Majjhima Nikaya:

> At last I came to a pleasant forest grove next to a river of
> pure water and sat down beneath a big tree, sure that this
> was the right place for realization.

By the way, you don't need the forest and the big tree to find realization; the Buddha just happened to do it that way.

> All the conditions of the world came into my mind, one

after another, and as they came they were penetrated and put down. In this way, finally, a knowledge and insight arose, and I knew this was the changeless, the unconditioned. This was freedom.

In other words, every time a mental construct of the world came into his head, he refused any mental or intellectual understanding of it. He refused any solution, any explanation, any knowledge, any wisdom. The Heart Sutra says, "No eye, ear, nose, tongue, body, mind. No form, sound, smell, taste, touch, phenomena." He got past every possible mental construction until he saw the empty nature of all things.

It sounds very fancy when you put it that way. But in another way, we could say that he accepted his life exactly as it was at that moment without separating from it. He became "one with." He was neither Buddhist nor Hindu, neither religious nor non-religious. There was no philosophy or concepts. After he got rid of all of that, there he was, an awakened being.

By negating everything, the Buddha deeply affirmed the reality that can't be accessed by words and concepts. He saw that "death" was a word for something, but he didn't know what it was. He saw that "life" was a word for something, but didn't know what it was. He saw that "body" and "mind" were words for things, but he didn't know what they were. He saw through every possible construction of the mind. The practice starts where concepts stop. "The reality that came to me is profound," the Buddha told us, "but it's hard to see or understand because it is beyond the sphere of thinking."

There's only one true person: a buddha. That's who you really are. If you go deep enough, that's the destination you're going to reach. That's where you're going to hit the ground of your own mind. If we think and think and think, we eventually get to the place where we ask ourselves, "Okay, what is it that's beyond concepts? What is it that's beyond thinking?" The Buddha says that what he found was sublime yet subtle. Indefinable, ungraspable, it can be attained only by the dedicated.

> If I were to try to teach this truth, this reality, nobody
> would understand me, I thought. My labor and my trouble
> would be for nothing.
> But then it came to me as an insight that I should teach
> this truth, for it is also happiness. There are people whose
> sight is only a little clouded and they are suffering through
> not hearing the reality. They would become knowers of the
> truth. It was in this way I went forth to teach.

The Buddha's solution was to embrace everything. He decided life was not the problem, or the question; it was the answer. Death was not the question; it was the answer. Impermanence was not the question; it was the answer. Contemplating impermanence, birth, and death are lifelong practices. We may know impermanence is an important aspect of reality, but living according to impermanence requires that we continually remind ourselves of it. And of course the answer, as always, is right in front of our noses.

When I was living in upstate New York, some genius opened an attraction called the World's Largest Kaleidoscope. Everybody in the neighborhood was grossly offended, especially those at the nearby monastery, because it was right in their backyard. It may not have been very spiritual, but it was wonderfully tacky. There was a fire engine that had been turned into a cafe, and a collection of funky, upstate New York odds and ends, lots of farm tools, little stables, outdoor furniture, and, best of all, a bunch of old fire engines parked in a kind of contrived disorder and acting as markers pointing the way to a restaurant serving upstate New York cuisine: hamburgers.

Caryn, Alex, and I decided to go check it out. We entered a dark room and sat down and leaned our heads back, like in a planetarium. We stared at the domed ceiling and waited for the show to begin. A little boy began yelling, "When does it start? When does it start?" Then the program started. The World's Biggest Kaleidoscope made nauseating circles on the ceiling, its colors shifting and folding and melting. Suddenly we heard the same kid again: "When does it stop? When does it stop?"

For most of us, this is life. We spend a good part of our lives wondering, "When does it start?" Then we're old and sick and dying, and we say, "When does it stop?" In the meantime we suffer. We create and are affected by karma, cause and effect. The reality of karma still exists even for the Awakened One. Karma is an impersonal law. Karma is just karma. Karma doesn't care.

On one level, we can say there is no karma. Nothing happens. When we're in touch with our awakened nature, there's no more cause and effect. When an Awakened One remembers who she is, she returns to what she was all along: being an Awakened One. Nothing ever happened, there has never been a problem. The Awakened One realizes more and more deeply that she is the Awakened One, and she can fly free. The world returns to the magical place it is. She doesn't have to sit around encumbered by the thought that the world is coming to an end, because the world didn't come to a beginning. Since the Awakened Mind is all that there is, we can be kind and caring; we can work and play well with others. Why do something that's going to make things unpleasant for people? They might make things unpleasant for you. The Majjhima Nikaya says:

> For those who are ready,
> the door to the deathless state is open.
> You that have ears,
> give up the conditions that bind you, and enter in.

Entering the deathless state is quite a tall order. The Buddha is saying that in order to wake up, we should give up our belief in death. That's the deathless state—giving up the belief that we know what a body is, that we know what a mind is.

The practice is simple and deep. It can appear to be boring and re-petitive, but the practice itself is not boring. When we free ourselves of thoughts like "life" and "death," it's not boring. Our conditioning runs deep. Our repetitive thoughts and feelings are really ingrained. Even when we see through our conditioning, we tend to claim this experience as a new concept. Because we keep creating new constructs, practice is ongoing, never-ending. This is not unusual in any kind of training. The classical pianist Arthur Rubenstein said that if he missed practice one day, he would notice the difference in his playing; if he missed two days, the music critics would notice; three days and his audience would notice.

I used to be really stuck in my belief that the practice was boring. For a while, Zen practice, especially meditation, was the ultimate torture. I used to sit there and think of every Chinese restaurant I'd ever eaten at just to get through a sitting period. One day it occurred to me that "I'm bored" and "When is this period going to end?" were simply thoughts. I was stuck in the hole.

> "You're thinking about something, my dear, and that makes you
> forget to talk. I can't tell you just now what the moral of that is,
> but I shall remember it in a bit."
> "Perhaps it hasn't one," Alice ventured to remark.
> "Tut, tut, child!" said the Duchess. "Everything's got a moral, if only
> you can find it."

The Buddha says teaching is difficult because it necessitates having learned and reflected on something. But awakening is not about learning something or thinking something. It's about waking up to this huge work, this huge game. In fact, you're in it. You look at it, and you're in it. It's called your life. It's the world's largest kaleidoscope.

So, what and who is the Awakened One? We have to stop worrying about trying to solve that question. To accept fully what is happening moment to moment, to not separate from it, is realization. It's not definable. It doesn't fall into a category. It's not sane or insane; it's just reality.

The Awakened One can't be characterized. As soon as we say "this is it" or "that is it," it loses its open, spacious, unknowable quality. The Awakened One takes to that quality like a duck to water. Reclaiming, being, and deepening ourselves as the Awakened One is our practice. Eventually, we become one with this open, spacious, unknowable life and death. And that is called awakening and freedom. The Majjhima Nikaya says:

> The mighty ocean has but one taste, the taste of salt. Even
> so, the true way has but one savor, the savor of freedom.

In the collection of early Buddhist sutras known as the Sutta Nipata, it says:

> Overcome your uncertainties and free yourself from dwell-
> ing on sorrow. If you delight in existence, you will become
> a guide to those who need you, revealing the path to many.

The Buddha probably started out thinking he was going to defeat problems. When he reached nirvana and became one with it, he relaxed. His quest, his ideas, his thoughts were extinguished. He saw *this* shore as the other shore, as the end of struggle. It's not complex. You just have to stop believing that you're going to solve the problem. That's why we practice. That is koan study. The ultimate truth of what the historical Buddha was searching for is being preached every moment. You can't grasp it; it's not a "thing." So we can relax and be tranquil. We can delight in life and death without grasping or trying to solve them. That is the sound of truth. The rest is conjecture.

Eight

TWO FRIES SHORT OF A HAPPY MEAL

"The rule is, jam tomorrow and jam yesterday—but never jam today."

"It must come sometimes to 'jam today,'" Alice objected.

"No, it can't," said the Queen. "It's jam every other day; today isn't any other day, you know."

—*Through the Looking Glass* by Lewis Carroll

*O*ne day I saw a bumper sticker on the back of a car that said, "Are you a few fries short of a happy meal?" It reminded me of what's being called "the supersizing of America"—for just a few cents more, consumers can get larger portions of food. We seem convinced that getting more of something is going to make us happier. I don't think we always consider what we want, what we have, or if any of this makes sense. Like Alice was doing before she fell through the hole, we are just going along with the conventional "wisdom" we have assimilated. We are striving to get those extra French fries and supersize our lives so we can have a happy meal.

Really, it's not such a happy meal. The other day, my wife and I were talking about something that was going to happen in our future, and I said, "In fifteen years we're going to be seventy." All of a sudden I heard myself saying: *In fifteen years we're going to be seventy?* Gee, that doesn't sound so good. Life can seem like a downhill ride.

In the meantime we go through life and things just keep getting worse. So we wish we were young again, forgetting that when we were young, we thought things were terrible then, too. It can be so dizzying, we don't allow ourselves time to think about what we really want. It's a double delusion: we think things are getting worse; and, at another point, we think things are getting better. It appears there aren't so many happy meals out there, after all.

The Buddha said that life is suffering. It's simply a reminder that we want life to be something other than what it is. We're always wanting something; a nicer car or a bigger TV. When we get the car or the TV we may feel better for a little while, but soon enough we want something else. Anything else. In other words, we never want "this," we want "that." More fries for more happy meals. We may define "that" differently throughout our lives. Perhaps "that" is money, sex, love, houses, vacations, or more popcorn. If we get more of "that," then "this" is going to be okay. But has it ever really happened? Have you ever gotten enough? Did you really need more in the first place? So why would we believe such foolishness? Instead of asking this question, we continue to consume the same happy meals again and again. This is what the fast food joints are counting on. Taking a big step to try to see things another way can be frightening. Like Alice, we learn caution early on.

It was all very well to say "Drink Me," but the wise little Alice was not going to do that in a hurry. "No, I'll look first," she said, "and see whether it's marked 'poison' or not," for she had read several nice little stories about children who had got burnt, and eaten up by wild beasts, and other unpleasant things, all because they would not remember the simple rules their friends had taught them.

Sometimes we have ideas about happiness—getting those extra fries—that we're not even conscious of. When I was around thirty and working as a musician, my fellow musicians and I all thought it would be great to make it big in the music business. For us, that was the ultimate happy meal. An old friend of my girlfriend at the time was married to a member of the band Pink Floyd, who had just put out a well-received album called *The Wall.* My girlfriend and I were invited to meet the band at their hotel in New York and accompany them to the concert they were giving. We rode to the concert hall in the band's limousine and hung out backstage with scores of famous musicians, artists, and models. Andy Warhol and his entourage were there, along with many others.

I was very excited when I arrived, but as the evening wore on I became more and more depressed. I had convinced myself that if happiness could be found anywhere, it would be here with these successful, artistic people. And that wasn't true at all. As celebrated as they were, these people's success came with an awful lot of baggage. It came as a huge shock to me. I stayed awake that night thinking about it for a long time; and finally I became free, free of something I hadn't even known was part of me.

Another experience I had as a musician also closed a door and freed me. I was playing with a band at a club in uptown Manhattan. We had done three encores and the audience was screaming for more. I realized that this energy, this wired intensity I once thought of as desirable, was not the way I wanted to live. All of this helped me see through my own illusions. It helped me see that things I had assumed would please me, wouldn't, and that I was operating under a lot of delusion. While I was anxious to get what I wanted, I didn't really know what that was, or even who I was.

"Well! WHAT are you?" said the Pigeon. "I can see you're trying to invent something!"

People are often drawn to Zen practice as a means of searching for enlightenment or realization, an opening where you see the true nature of the self. Imagine you are a wave in the ocean. You're rolling along thinking, "I'm a wave called Daniel." But maybe you don't like your shape. You'd like to be a little taller, a little thinner. The other waves are getting too close to you. You don't like your place in the ocean. None of these things are really your fault. This is a thing we call karma. The moon is pulling, the wind is blowing, the other waves are slapping up against you, and that's giving you the shape you don't like. That's what we call suffering. Furthermore, you can see the shore where the waves all crash and end and you're afraid. As you get closer to the shore, you loosen your grip and peter out. Now the whole thing is ocean. No wave.

Through practice, a simple but profound thing happens. You realize that you are the ocean and not just the wave. The wave was always nothing more than ocean. There is no wave that is not ocean. If you are a wave, you are also the ocean. The Japanese call this experience of glimpsing the simple truth, *kensho*. Enlightenment is when you catch a glimpse of kensho and see it deeply, and then it stays with you, so that you walk around unable to forget that you're the ocean as well as the wave. Enlightenment can become more and more lucid. It never ends. What might begin to end is the feeling that you are missing something. Like those fries.

Then comes embodiment, the second part of the practice. A person who has realized she is the ocean begins to behave like the ocean. How does the ocean behave differently than a wave? When you're a wave and you don't know you're also the ocean, the other waves irritate you and you elbow them out of the way. When you are the ocean, you realize that all the waves are you. The urge to get more, and the lack of appreciation for what is and who we are loses its potency. Like Alice, we gradually—sometimes clumsily and sometimes graciously—accept this new reality we've dropped into.

Enlightenment ends the strong karma. Enlightenment ends the illusion that you know who you are. Enlightenment ends the suffering caused by thinking that you are an alienated being living in a strange place, dying and becoming dust. You're emancipated. You're free.

When you're on this path and your realizations become clearer and deeper, there will be ups and downs. There will be times when you see your true nature clearly, but you don't feel connected to it. "I see my true nature, so why am I acting like this?" There are going to be many moments like that. But emancipation is freeing. A student having the first opening experience that happens with the first koan will often cry. Seeing our true nature is deeply pleasurable.

Our ancestors in the Zen lineage came up with a profound idea: if "that" was never going to make "this" better, then what about "this"? Can being with "this" make "this" better? And the answer is, "Yes!" The experience that the Buddha calls "realization" or "enlightenment" is simply being "this." You can think of it as maturity. Maybe you're growing older and you think you should run out and get Botox or liposuction. But railing against age and being grouchy and bitter about it is like being a two-year-old having a tantrum. A secret of this practice is that being with what is transforms us.

Koans are like questions or encounters; you have to understand and present your understanding of them in a one-on-one meeting with your teacher. You don't explain the koan. It's an intuitive understanding that is not expressed with words. It's the way we make realization expand and continue.

In this koan from *The Gateless Gate*, or *Mumonkan*, one of the two most important collections of koans in Zen literature, we meet Seppo and Ganto, two famous students of Master Tokusan. This story takes place after they've both become renowned teachers.

When Seppo was living in his hermitage, two monks came to pay their respects. As Seppo saw them coming, he pushed open the gate and presented himself before them saying, "What is this?" The monks also said, "What is this?" Seppo lowered his head and returned to his cottage. Later the monks came to Ganto who said, "Where are you from?" The monks answered, "We have come from south of Nanray Mountain." Ganto said, "Have you seen Seppo?" The monks said, "Yes" and told him what happened. "Alas," he said, "I regret that I did not tell him the last word of Zen when I was with him. If I had done so, no one in the world could have pretended to outdo him." At the end of the summer sesshin, the monks repeated the story and asked Ganto for his instruction. Ganto said, "Why didn't you ask earlier?" The monks said, "We had a hard time struggling with it." Ganto said, "Seppo was born on the same stem as I, but he will not die on the same stem. If you want to know the last word, it is just this. This is it. This is it."

So two monks, who have been practicing a long time, go to Seppo asking for the deepest instruction. And Seppo says to them, "What is this?" That's the deepest thing he can tell them about the practice. *What is this?* Look around. Are we on the planet Earth? Those are words. Are we in our heads? Are we out of our heads? Are we having a dream? Are we alive? Are we dead? Where are we? What is this?

The deepest question. And the monks answer, "What is this?" because they understand.

Then they go to brother Ganto and tell him what happened. Ganto says, "Good. Good. That's good." They stick around and they don't ask anything further. But in the end, they ask him what his deepest instruction is. He doesn't say, "What is this?" He says, "This is it."

And he says, "Even though Seppo and I came to life on the same tree, we do not die in the same way." Coming to life on the same tree means having the same teacher, Master Tokusan. To die is to die as a wave and return to the ocean. The way Seppo returns to the ocean is, "What is this?" The way Ganto returns is, "This is it." They are two sides to one truth. They both die as a wave, but they die in two different ways. If we forget everything we know—Buddha, dharma, Zen, name, gender, age, religion, race, size, shape, and history—there is only one thing left: this. When a person reaches a state where she's not looking for more fries to make a happy meal, being one with what is, that's enlightenment. That's the beginning. As Seppo and Ganto indicate, this is it, and nobody knows what this is.

Do you hear the birds singing outside? Do the sound waves reach your ears? Is the sound from the birds launched through space like a baseball right into your ears? Do you really hear that sound with your ears? I'm not sure how I hear that sound.

When you dive into the cold water on a spring day, is "cold water" what you experience? Try to describe cold water to someone who's never jumped into cold water. It doesn't work. Like any unfettered experience, cold water is difficult to describe. We've dropped into a crazy hole and we keep trying to understand everything we're seeing, but that's not what we or Alice really need. We need to get with the program: to fall, drop, fly.

Then turn not pale, beloved snail, but come and join the dance.

There's something else we know but that we don't trust. We keep looking for something else even while we're already experiencing something wonderful. I named my own Zen group Lost Coin after a parable that appears in Christian and Buddhist sources about being poor and not knowing we have a coin of great value in our pocket—ourselves.

Yet, we cannot live without desires and goals; even the desire to practice, to realize ourselves, is a goal. So this is part of our lives. Maybe the real question is, can we pursue our lives and our practice while not practicing "stepladder Zen," understanding that every step of the way is the way.

It's not sane to believe that what life is constantly showing us is not true. Sooner or later, life will knock us off that belief. I went through this mindset, and I'm still going through it. If it's possible, I used to be stupider than I am now. At the beginning of my adult life, everything shocked me. When I got married, I thought I'd be happily married forever after. Then my wife died. I got married again and then I got divorced and it shocked me. Now I've been very happily married to my wife Caryn for twenty-seven years. What a wonderful surprise. I didn't expect that either. Isn't it incredibly naive to think that bad things don't happen to everyone? To think that in all of history bad things happen only to certain people?

There's another way to approach things. That way is to wake up from the dream of good and bad things happening, and instead to realize that we are a wave and that we are also the ocean. Waves crash and spill, they come in and out of existence. From the ocean's point of view, this is neither good nor bad. It's just ocean. We're just ocean.

The person responsible for many of the Zen traditions as we know them is Eno, the Sixth Patriarch. As a young man, he was a poor, illiterate woodcutter. Then he heard somebody recite the Diamond Sutra and boom! His mind opened. The part of the Diamond Sutra that always sticks with me is when the Buddha says to Subhuti, "This world is not a world. Therefore, it is provisionally called a world." Think about that. When we say, "the world," it has all kinds of connotations. It's Brooklyn, it's New Orleans, it's Poughkeepsie. But is that true of this world? No! Everything is this world.

Where is the end of your mind? Is there a difference between this world and your mind? No. Our mind and this world are the same thing. World and mind are one, and in oneness there's no subject and no object. We call that Buddha nature. The world mind. One thing. Waves and ocean.

Zen practice is just sanity, waking up. What's important in life? This! You come to a practice center in the morning, and you think about going to sit in the zendo. That is Zen practice, but it's not really Zen practice. Real Zen practice is when one foot hits the floor, and the floor is realized—completely. The other foot hits the floor, and the floor is realized completely. You light the incense; incense is everything. You smell the incense; that is your life. There's no life anywhere else. That, and you pay your taxes and you walk your dog in Wonderland.

Dogen Zenji clearly states that the most important part of understanding the ocean is that the ocean is not a word. "Realization" is a word, but the experience is not a word. "Life" is a word, but the experience is not a word. "I'll be seventy in fifteen years" is a thought. Something will happen, but not that. "This is a world" is a concept. "Death" is a concept. There's something else going on here besides words. That thing is one thing, and you are that one thing. That's the ocean. Through practice, anybody can realize this way of seeing.

All worrying is based on knowing—I'm going to go bankrupt, I'll be out on the streets, then I'll get a disease, then I'll be in a box in the ground looking at the box top, my family will probably have bought me a cheap one, the ants will be coming in, and I'll be worried about it. Or worse yet, I'll get cremated and wind up in heaven without a body, or in a little box stored on a mantelpiece.

This is how I think sometimes. But do I actually know any of this? Does any of this actually happen in that way? Do we know where we're going? If we don't know, it's okay, we can forget about it. Yet we need to take care of the separate individual self that is just a bunch of worries, fears, and anxieties, and having your feelings hurt by others because they didn't notice your new haircut. Through our practices, we become more familiar with the true self and we can develop more perspective and compassion for everything that is and everything we are as well, bad haircut included.

The self is our conditioning that we constantly reinforce through our thoughts and feelings. We have been programmed with so much that we take for granted.

> "I'm sure I'm not Ada," she said, "for her hair goes in such long ringlets, and mine doesn't go in ringlets at all; and I'm sure I can't be Mabel, for I know all sorts of things, and she, oh! she knows such a very little! Besides, SHE'S she, and I'm I, and—oh dear, how puzzling it all is! I'll try if I know all the things I used to know."

I started spiritual practice when I was seventeen, with a group that practiced the Fourth Way based on the teachings of Gurdjieff and Ouspensky. After several years I decided I wanted to become more deeply involved with the Gurdjieff Foundation. A musician who had been involved with the foundation gave me a phone number to call. There was some secrecy involved and it all seemed rather magical. Every week at the same time I called the number and asked to meet the person from the foundation. Each week I was told to call back next week at the same time. I understood that my seriousness was being tested, but I knew what I wanted and I was determined. Finally, after a year of phone calls, a mysterious person named James Wycoff agreed to see me. We met in the Barbizon Hotel in New York. I waited in the lobby nervously until James showed up, and then we went down the street to a coffee shop on Lexington Avenue. After some conversation, he looked right at me and said, "Now what do you want?" Thirty-five years later, when I received transmission from Genpo Roshi, he told me he had one final koan for me. I asked what it was. He said, "What do you want?"

> "How fond she is of finding morals in things!" Alice thought to herself.
> "I quite agree with you," said the Duchess; "and the moral of that
> is—'Be what you would seem to be'—or if you'd like it put more
> simply—'Never imagine yourself not to be otherwise than what it
> might appear to others that what you were or might have been
> was not otherwise than what you had been would have appeared
> to them to be otherwise.'"

Perfectly clear, right? That's what going down into the hole will do to you.

When we think about sitting meditation, there's a tendency to think, "Okay, I'm going to get down on my cushion and arrange my hands and sit there. God, that's going to be boring." If you think that's boring, wake up in the middle of the night and start worrying—see how boring that is. Sitting is not boring. You just have to learn how to do it. After you sit for a while, you forget about finding those extra fries. You realize you don't need to supersize; you're already quite happy enough. When we realize our identity—our intimacy with the world, with the One Mind—we find we are exactly the right size, which is no size. Pass the ketchup, please. All the bad dreams start to fade away. Your parents' dreams, the government's dreams, the other government's dreams, the corporation's dreams—all the dreams recede until we reach that place the Heart Sutra describes:

> No eye, ear, nose, tongue, body, mind, no color, sound,
> smell, taste, touch, phenomena, no realm of sight, no realm
> of consciousness, no ignorance, no end to ignorance, no old
> age and death, no end to old age and death, no suffering,
> no cause of suffering, no extinguishing, no path, no wis-
> dom, no gain.

And thus the bodhisattva lives *"prajña paramita"* which means deep wisdom. And then, *"Gate gate paragate parasamgate bodhisvaha,"* which means, "gone, gone, gone to the other shore," which is this shore. "Gone far beyond," and then *"svaha,"* which means, "yippee!"

Zazen is a way to stop our exhausting rat race for a moment. I'm putting it in modern terms, but I don't think the historical Buddha would mind. When asked if he was a god, the Buddha said no. A sage? No. A saint? No. Well then, what? And he said, "I am awake. I teach the end of suffering."

Will you won't you, will you won't you, won't you join the dance?

We now have a 2,500-year-old lineage teaching the end of suffering. But it's not only about suffering. A lesson of Mahayana Buddhism is that we don't end all our suffering and then go up into the hills and enjoy ourselves. Our enlightenment is not for ourselves alone. Saving all sentient beings is a group effort, a sangha effort, a world effort. It starts with each one of us and extends out. Every time you sit, it's something you do for the world. Every time you sit, you affect the world. That's because we're the ocean, and what we do vibrates throughout the entire ocean. But that's true only if you realize it, only if you make the effort to do it, only if you practice. You will not realize it without practice—sincere practice.

We don't say, "Believe this" and we don't say, "Believe that." We don't say, "This is this way!" and we don't say, "That is that way!" Instead, we say, "We don't know." This is a practice, not a philosophy. I think we are all looking for the happy meal, for Wonderland, and for enlightenment, which is nothing other than being awake in every moment of our lives.

Will you, won't you, will you, won't you, will you join the dance?

Dogen Zenji is the most famous teacher in our particular Buddhist lineage. He traveled from Japan to China in the thirteenth century. He traveled far and practiced long and hard, and was told many meaningful things. Finally he experienced what his Chinese teacher taught to his students: "Body and mind dropped off." Dogen dropped it all: all the thoughts, all the concepts, everything he had been taught about who he was. The ground gave way and he fell all the way down the hole. He experienced, deeply, what is never lost: our limitless life and death—Wonderland.

Lastly, she pictured to herself how this same little sister of hers would, in the after-time, be herself a grown woman; and how she would keep, through all her riper years, the simple and loving heart of her childhood: and how she would gather about her other little children, and make their eyes bright and eager with many a strange tale, perhaps even with the dream of Wonderland of long ago.

ABOUT THE AUTHOR

$\mathcal{D}$aniel Doen Silberberg Sensei was born in Bad Hartzburg, Germany, in 1947 and moved to New York City when he was four. Doen Sensei began spiritual practice with teachers in the Gurdjieff lineage at the age of seventeen. He was appointed by the late Willem Nyland to teach a Gurdjieff group in Woodstock, New York, when he was thirty-two.

Doen Sensei began formal Zen practice under John Daido Loori Roshi and then-Abbot Hakuyu Taizan Maezumi Roshi at Zen Mountain Monastery in Mt. Tremper, New York. There he met Caryn Shudo Schlessinger. They were married in 1982 by Maezumi Roshi. Doen Sensei met Genpo Merzel Roshi in 1980 and became his formal student in 1994. He received *shiho*, dharma transmission, from Genpo Roshi in December 2003.

Doen Sensei is the former vice abbot of Kanzeon Zen Center in Salt Lake City, Utah. He received a BA in English and a PhD in psychology. He has had a successful career as a musician, psychotherapist, coach, and consultant. He currently teaches and directs his own Zen group, Lost Coin, which has students throughout the U.S. and Europe.

Doen Sensei would like to thank Ann Floor, Julie Reiser, and Rachel Neumann whose efforts and literary abilities made this book possible, Genpo Roshi and Daido Roshi for showing me the Way, and Caryn Shudo Silberberg and Alex Schlessinger for giving me a reason to believe.

Parallax Press, a nonprofit organization, publishes books on engaged
Buddhism and the practice of mindfulness by Thich Nhat Hanh and other
authors. All of Thich Nhat Hanh's work is available at our online store and
in our free catalog. For a copy of the catalog, please contact:

PARALLAX PRESS
P.O. Box 7355
Berkeley, CA 94707
Tel: (510) 525-0101
www.parallax.org

Monastics and laypeople practice the art of mindful living in the tradition of
Thich Nhat Hanh at retreat communities in France and the United States.
To reach any of these communities, or for information about individuals and
families joining for a practice period, please contact:

PLUM VILLAGE
13 Martineau
33580 Dieulivol, France
www.plumvillage.org

BLUE CLIFF MONASTERY
3 Mindfulness Road
Pine Bush, NY 12566
www.bluecliffmonastery.org

DEER PARK MONASTERY
2499 Melru Lane
Escondido, CA 92026
www.deerparkmonastery.org

The Mindfulness Bell, a journal of the art of mindful living in the tradition of
Thich Nhat Hanh, is published three times a year by Plum Village.
To subscribe or to see the worldwide directory of Sanghas, visit
www.mindfulnessbell.org